HIP Readers' Theater Plays

By Paul Kropp and Lori Jamison

For grades 4 to 10 | Easy to read and perform
With teaching and performance notes

High Interest Publishing | HIP Books

Copyright © 2007 by High Interest Publishing, Inc.
407 Wellesley Street East
Toronto, Ontario M4X 1H5
Canada

High Interest Publishing is an imprint of the Chestnut Publishing Group.

High Interest Publishing acknowledges the financial support of the Government of Canada
through the Book Publishing Industry Development Program (BPIDP) for our publishing
activities.

Library and Archives Canada Cataloguing in Publication

Kropp, Paul, 1948–
    HIP readers' theater plays / by Paul Kropp and Lori Jamison.
"For grades 4 to 10; easy to read and perform; with teaching and performance notes".

ISBN 978-1-897039-40-3

1. Readers' theater. 2. Oral reading. 3. Children's plays,
Canadian (English) 4. Reading (Elementary) 5. Reading (Middle
school) I. Jamison, Lori, 1955– II. Title.

PS8571.R772H46 2007   372.66'044   C2007-901269-8

Designer: Laura Brady
Cover design: Robert Corrigan

1 2 3 4 5 6 7   12 11 10 09 08 07

Printed and bound in Canada by SpreadInk

Table of Contents

READERS' THEATER PLAYS

Introduction

Readers' Theater is a technique for performing an unstaged play from a prepared script. The script is often based on a picture book, novel or story but may sometimes offer dramatic representations of speeches, essays or science concepts. Generally speaking, no costumes, sets or props are used in the performance. Instead, student actors use their voices, facial expressions and sound effects to create a convincing dramatic experience. Often a narrator conveys the story's setting and provides any necessary transition between scenes.

Obviously, Readers' Theater offers a good introduction to drama by magically transforming the classroom into a stage. But Readers' Theater is far more than a classroom exercise in dramatic arts. Many studies show it to be a powerful tool for building key reading skills.

Readers' Theater develops comprehension by requiring readers to understand characters and situations. It builds fluency through repeated reading and rehearsal of a script. It engages both participants and audience in the reading and performance of a shared text. And it builds confidence in even the most reluctant reader.

In Readers' Theater, the script is read rather than memorized. To do this effectively, student readers need to practise and rehearse carefully to depict the characters and convey the message of the play.

The performance of a Readers' Theater requires a reader/performer to rehearse his or her role many times, individually and as part of the ensemble. A reader might well rehearse his or her role 20 times before the actual performance to effectively portray the character and the emotions in the play. Each individual role must be practised until it is read fluently, and then the entire performance (with sound effects) must be rehearsed until the presentation is seamless and effective. Only then can the magic of theater transform students into characters, their classmates into an engaged audience, and your classroom into a theater.

In his book *The Fluent Reader,* researcher Tim Rasinski says, "Readers' theater is an authentic, entertaining, and educationally powerful way to communicate meaning." Rasinski offers extensive research support for the use of prepared oral reading in the classroom:

- Students enjoy reading more.
- Students explore more sophisticated words and text structures.
- Students build oral reading confidence and fluency.
- Students become a community of oral readers.

Rasinski's own findings reported a gain of 17 words per minute in fluency, and significant improvements in comprehension, among students who engaged in Readers' Theater for

<1>

<2 Recording Readers' Theater>

just ten weeks. "We are gaining evidence from classroom research that Readers' Theater yields improvements in students' word recognition, fluency and comprehension."

The key, of course, is repeated reading of the same material. With each visit to a piece of familiar text, readers build fluency, comprehension and confidence. Readers' Theater takes advantage of this key reading practice by providing readers with an opportunity for performance.

Recording Readers' Theater

Some students prefer to make a tape or digital recording of a Readers' Theater performance. This takes away some of the pressure of a "live" performance in front of a classroom audience. Recording also makes it possible to record the play in a series of "takes" so that the final audio represents a best effort by the group even if they've had to re-record the script many times.

The problems with recording a production are two: time required and technical issues. First, students often need many takes and retakes to record a performance at a level they find satisfactory. This can add hours and even days to allotted classroom time. Second, schools rarely have the sophisticated audio equipment used by the producers of books on tape and commercial audio. Students can spend a great deal of time striving for audio effects that are too difficult to achieve with the equipment at hand, or they may end up using their home computers to lay down tracks of voice and sound effects. Such ambitious production can yield superior results, but the time and effort required has limited educational value.

From an educational perspective, both live performance and recorded performance have their strengths. A live performance is closer to real theater: whatever happens, the show must go on. A taped performance can still be played to the entire class and frequently leads to even more re-reading than Readers' Theater ordinarily requires. As we have noted earlier, this is valuable for developing fluency and comprehension.

Ultimately, the choice of "live" versus "recorded" is up to the classroom teacher. That choice may differ from group to group, year to year, classroom to classroom.

<HIP Readers' Theater Scripts 3>

HIP Readers' Theater Scripts

The Readers' Theater scripts in this book are all adapted from sections of HIP Sr. and HIP Jr. novels. Although the novels are designed for students reading below grade level, the authentic dialogue and exciting plots make these scripts appropriate for any reader. These scripts may be used as "stand-alone" reading and drama activities in their own right, or they may be used as introductions to the HIP novels, establishing a context for the book and enticing students to read. In other situations, the scripts may be used as follow-up activities to the reading of the novels, to develop comprehension, improve fluency and develop reading confidence.

Although it is possible for teachers and students to create their own Readers' Theater scripts, this task is more challenging than it might seem. The HIP Readers' Theater scripts have been professionally developed and classroom tested. They feature:

- a consistent level of reading difficulty to support less capable readers
- five to six speaking roles of equal length in most scripts
- carefully selected typeface and design to minimize miscues at line breaks and maximize readability for accurate reading and acting

- sound effects to extend the number of participants or engage the audience in participating in the performance

In addition, special supports are provided for the teacher. These include background information for the script, a synopsis of the original novel, performance notes and teaching tips. All of these scripts have been tested in actual classrooms and the scripts revised to anticipate problems that students might encounter in production.

The High Interest Publishing website at www.hip-books.com offers a number of resources that can be used to help teach Readers' Theater. There are pages to help organize groups, rubrics for marking productions and downloadable audio samples of actual students reading plays. As well, new plays are always being developed for the newest HIP novels, so teachers may want to download these in their trial editions for use with their students.

Note: In our testing, we've found that a teacher can effectively take one of the narrator roles. This keeps the drama moving forward and provides a model of phrasing and intonation.

<4 Teaching Readers' Theater>

Teaching Readers' Theater

One important finding from recent research into teaching language arts will come as little surprise: teachers must spend time teaching and modeling for their students. Readers' Theater is no exception.

As adults, teachers are familiar with many of the conventions of theater and reading scripts. Students, however, may never have seen live theater and often have little experience reading a script for dramatic performance. Before students attempt Readers' Theater themselves, it is essential to teach the important conventions of script reading and to practise some aspects of dramatic performance.

A script has certain conventions not found in other literary forms. These should be taught to students as the teacher models (or does a thinkaloud) through one of the scripts.

- The name of the CHARACTER who speaks each line is written first (all in capital letters for these scripts), occasionally followed by an instruction on how to deliver a line and then followed by the line itself. Neither the character nor the instruction is ever voiced, only the line itself.

- Sometimes a line is interrupted with an instruction. For instance, *(pause)* would indicate a break in the speaking. An instruction like *(sarcastic)* indicates how a line should be spoken. An instruction like *(whispering to Ryan)* indicates that only one character should hear the line.

- Some lines have sound effects interspersed with the text. For instance, *(sound effect: thump)* shows what kind of sound should be performed with the spoken text. When the sound effects are on a separate line, the sound should be made *between* the spoken lines of dialogue. For some plays, the sound effects are so important that a student might be assigned just to perform them. Any sound effect should continue for some natural duration: thunder is momentary but wind noise would be oingoing.

- Sometimes a word or a phrase will be set in italics. This usually means that the word or phrase receives more emphasis than the others in that sentence.

MUSIC BEFORE AND AFTER: Students very much enjoy selecting music to lead into a Readers' Theater play and to act as a concluding song at the end. There is some learning in selecting music appropriate to the theme and mood of a play, but don't let the search for tunes or downloads interfere with the main goal of performance.

<Preparing a Readers' Theater Performance 5>

Preparing a Readers' Theater Performance

There are eight steps to preparing and presenting a Readers' Theater performance:

1. **First read** – Each student should read through the entire script to get an overall sense of the story and the characters. Teachers will find performance notes, teaching tips and a summary of the original novel from which the script is excerpted in the introduction to each script.

2. **Role assignment** – Roles can be assigned by random selection or by asking for volunteers. If more than one student is interested in performing a role, a teacher should make an educated choice or draw straws. Auditioning for roles is not efficient or productive use of class time, especially for struggling readers.

3. **Script marking** – It is helpful for each reader to go through the script and highlight his or her speaking parts. Readers may also want to add performance notes (e.g., underline words to special emphasis or effect, note pauses or sound effects) for their own use.

4. **Individual practice** – Repeated practice is the key to a successful Readers' Theater experience. Students should practise their own parts orally, by themselves, until they can read the script fluently and expressively. This will ensure that they do not stumble over words when reading their parts in front of the rest of the group.

5. **Group practice** – After all the students have had an opportunity to practise their parts, the group should come together to rehearse the entire script. The group must work together to make some decisions about how the script will be read. Are there certain words that should be emphasized? Should some phrases be read more loudly or softly, more slowly or more quickly? Should there be pauses for effect or to add suspense? How will the sound effects come into the play - and for how long? Cooperation is essential in preparing for the presentation. As a group, students should work on timing, expression and enunciation. Transitions between speakers should be seamless, especially when one speaker is called upon to "interrupt" another speaker. Page turns should not interfere with the action or flow of the dialogue. In general, students should strive for as professional a performance as they can manage.

6. **Final touches** – Only after the reading is polished and prepared should final touches, such as music or recorded sound effects, be added to enhance the performance. (Sometimes students will need a reminder that these are secondary to the dramatic reading itself.)

7. **"Dress" Rehearsal** – Although Readers' Theater does not require "dress" of any kind, it is a good idea for students to do a final run-through of the entire presentation, without stops, before they attempt a live performance in front of the class. This will help them learn how to cover mistakes during the actual performance.

8. **Performance** – And on with the show! With solid preparation, students should be able to perform any of these scripts with considerable success.

> It is essential to model and demonstrate these activities before expecting students to undertake a Readers' Theater performance on their own. Walk through a Readers' Theater script with the whole class before assigning the task to groups.

<Teaching Students to Read Orally 7>

Teaching Students to Read Orally

Performance reading is not like speaking and requires much more preparation than simply reading aloud. In ordinary speech, speakers may slur words, hesitate in mid-thought, repeat themselves or make corrections halfway through a sentence. Performance reading does not allow for any of these things unless the character's role calls for them.

Many students, especially struggling readers, are unaccustomed to reading aloud or they may be uncomfortable doing so. They often read mechanically, word by word, without phrasing or expression. Sometimes they rush through the text, without pausing appropriately at punctuation. Many students today do not enunciate words clearly. All of these skills must be explicitly taught in preparation for effective Readers' Theater or other forms of dramatic presentation, especially if the finished presentations will be performed for an adult audience.

Speed and Clarity

Oral reading may require some students to slow down their speed of speaking. Many young people speak very quickly and slur their speech. In performance reading, each word must be enunciated clearly. This does not mean word-by-word reading – in fact, phrasing is critical in effective oral reading – but it does require reading for meaning.

The pace of reading will depend on the text, the character and the emotional context of the scene. Most readers will pick up speed with rehearsal, but clarity of speech is always the most important consideration.

With some students, it sometimes helps to start with "robot reading" to emphasize articulation of every word. Put a short section of text, such as this sample from *Caught in the Blizzard* on the board or overhead. Read it together with your class, enunciating each word carefully and mechanically, without expression.

At last, Sam and Annie found Connor lying on the snow. Connor's snowmobile was broken. Connor was shivering from the cold.

Then revisit the text and work together to decide where it should be broken into phrases. (The punctuation marks are good clues.) For instance, a reading of

At last Sam . . . and Annie found Connor lying . . . on the snow.

makes little sense and would surely confuse the audience. Your students will enjoy practising other nonsensical approaches to phrasing to understand that the most effective reading would be

<8 Teaching Students to Read Orally>

*At last . . . Sam and Annie found Connor . . .
lying on the snow.*

Punctuation

Punctuation marks are traffic signals for readers. Periods are stop signs, an indication for the reader to pause because a thought is completed. Commas, colons and semi-colons are like yield signs: pause briefly and proceed with caution. Exclamation marks and question marks not only indicate meaning but also give the reader clues about how to use his or her voice.

Have students practise reading the following sentence in different ways by interpreting the punctuation.

> I won the lottery.
> I won the lottery!
> I won the lottery?

Note how punctuation changes the meaning of the following sentence:

> Woman without her man is nothing.
> Woman! Without her, man is nothing.

In Readers' Theater scripts, a line will sometimes end with a dash. This indicates that the speaker's line has been cut off by the next line. In performance, the next speaker might well begin even before the first speaker is finished. Similarly, there are times when two characters speak at once. These need not be entirely simultaneous, but should overlap each other.

Expression

Expression, emphasis, volume and tone are the elements that make oral reading engaging for an audience. Many students (and adults) are uncomfortable with expressive reading, especially when a text requires exaggerated expression. Taking on a role in Readers' Theater sometimes helps them overcome that discomfort. (Sometimes it is helpful to identify the characters with signs, hats or other props that enable the reader to "hide behind" the role.)

Have students practise reading sections of text, emphasizing different words each time, and discuss how the meaning of the text changes with different emphases.

> Don't say that to *me!*
> Don't say *that* to me!
> Don't *say* that to me!

Also practise reading a section of text with different expression and tone to convey different meanings. For example, the script for *The Crash* includes this line:

> *Nah, I'm trying to get you out.*

How would that line sound different if the character were angry, secretive, fearful or amused? How would it sound different if the actor were saying it to a small child, the school principal, a police officer?

> **Teaching students to read with expression and phrasing builds fluency and engagement with reading. Fluent readers read more, read better and read with more enjoyment.**

<Sources and Resources 9>

Sources and Resources

Sources

Lila Carrick provides a good online overview of Readers' Theater, along with a number of sources for scripts, at <www.reading.org/electronic/carrick>

Generally regarded as the best online source for free Readers' Theater scripts is the Aaron Shepard website:
<www.aaronshep.com/rt>

A good source for scripts for younger students is <www.teachingheart.net/readerstheater.htm>

Resources

Allington, Richard. *What Really Matters for Struggling Readers*. Allyn and Bacon, 2000 and 2004.

Rasinski, Timothy, Padak, N. et al. "Is reading fluency a key for successful high school reading?" *Journal of Adolescent and Adult Literacy* (2005), 49, 1, 12-27.

Rasinski, Timothy. *The Fluent Reader*. Scholastic, 2003.

Rasinski, Timothy. "Speed does matter in reading," *The Reading Teacher* (2000) 54, 146-151.

Samuels, SJ. "The method of repeated readings," *The Reading Teacher* (1979), 32, 403-408.

HIP Readers' Theater Scripts

These scripts have been arranged by interest and topic beginning with scripts for junior grades and ending with scripts most appropriate for junior and senior high school. Scripts range from Choose Your Bully, *appropriate for classes in grades 3 to 8, to* Juvie, *which is best suited for students in grades 7 and higher. All these scripts, like the novels from which they have been adapted, have reading levels between grades 2.5 and 3.5.*

<Choose Your Bully 13>

Choose Your Bully

Richard and Ling have been dealing with a bully all year long. Now Ling is mad enough to take him on – all by herself.

APPROPRIATE GRADE LEVELS: 3–8

PERFORMANCE TIME: 4 minutes

THE NOVEL IN BRIEF: Ling and Richard come up with a great idea to deal with their school bully – hire a bodyguard. But when their bodyguard starts to bully them too, they have to come up with a better scheme.

PERFORMING NOTES: The voices are key to a successful performance. Richard must be scared, Ling forceful and Chuck brutish. All sound effects can be made by the student actors themselves.

CHARACTERS:
Narrator 1 (9 lines)
Narrator 2 (9 lines)
Ling (9 lines)
Richard (5 lines)
Chuck – a bully (11 lines)

SOUND EFFECTS: *footsteps, thumps, laughter*

<14   Choose Your Bully>

Choose Your Bully – Readers' Theater

Narrator 1
Narrator 2
Ling
Richard
Chuck – a bully

SOUND EFFECTS: *footsteps, thumps, laughter*

NARRATOR 1:   This Readers' Theater play is adapted from the novel *Choose Your Bully* by Lori Jamison. Today's actors are

_____

_____

_____

NARRATOR 2:   Richard and Ling were walking to school. They were talking about Chuck, the school bully.

LING: You have to stop being a victim, Richard.

RICHARD: So how do I do that?

LING: Stand up for yourself.

RICHARD: Easy for you to say.

LING: Don't give in like a wuss. Tell Chuck no and just keep saying no.

NARRATOR 1:   Richard shook his head, then he looked ahead. There was Chuck, the bully, waiting for them.

(sound effect: footsteps)

CHUCK: Ah . . . Richie Rich, you are right on time. I need some lunch money.

<Choose Your Bully 15>

NARRATOR 2:	The three of them just stared at each other. Ling could feel all her muscles get tight.
RICHARD:	I don't have any money today.
CHUCK:	Yeah, like I really believe that. You've got more money than any kid in this town. Now pay up, or get beat up.
NARRATOR 1:	Ling tried to stand up for her friend.
LING:	Richard said no. And no means no.
CHUCK:	Shut up . . . Ding-a-Ling. This is between Richie Rich and me. You want to use this sidewalk, you've got to pay the toll. Unless you want to pay the toll for him.
LING:	There is no such thing as a toll sidewalk.
CHUCK:	I said shut up, Ling.
NARRATOR 2:	Chuck turned back to Richard and held out his hand.
CHUCK:	Two bucks today, kid.
RICHARD:	I . . . I don't have two bucks. I've only got fifty cents.
CHUCK:	That'll do, for a start.
NARRATOR 1:	Richard took off his backpack to look for money. That's when Ling got really angry.
LING:	Richard, don't give him anything!
CHUCK:	Shut up, Ling.
LING:	I mean it, Richard. You don't have to pay this jerk. This is robbery. This is theft. I'm going to call the cops.
CHUCK:	*(laughing)* With what?

<16 Choose Your Bully>

NARRATOR 2: Neither Richard nor Ling had a cell phone. Chuck had broken Richard's cell weeks ago.

NARRATOR 1: Richard found two quarters in his backpack and gave them to Chuck.

CHUCK: I'll take the lunch, too.

RICHARD: Hey, you said . . .

NARRATOR 2: That's when Ling lost it. She took off her backpack, holding it by the two shoulder straps.

NARRATOR 1: Then she lifted the backpack and whacked Chuck on his back! *(sound effect: thump!)*

NARRATOR 2: And she whacked him again! *(sound effect: thump!)*

NARRATOR 1: For a second, Chuck was too stunned to do much. Then he grabbed Ling's backpack and threw it to the ground. Laughing, he kicked it away. *(sound effect: Chuck laughing)*

NARRATOR 2: So Ling came at him with her fists. She got a good hit into his shoulder before Chuck grabbed her hands.

LING: So what now, Chuck? You going to hit a . . . girl?

CHUCK: Keep it up and I will.

LING: *(mocking him)* What a man! *(pause)* What a jerk!

NARRATOR 1: Then Chuck got angry. He soon answered Ling's question.

NARRATOR 2: No, Chuck would *not* hit a girl. But he'd sure give a girl one big push.

CHUCK: *(grunt)*

NARRATOR 1: Ling went flying backwards and landed on her butt.

(sound effect: thump)

LING: You jerk!

CHUCK: *(laughter)*

NARRATOR 2: Chuck picked up Richard's lunch and walked off to school.

NARRATOR 1 and 2: That's when Ling knew that something – something! – had to be done about this.

(closing music)

Bats in the Graveyard

A Halloween thriller! Sam and Simon (the Bat Gang) have gone to a graveyard to deal with a group of bullies. Soon they face a growling dog and a terrifying ghoul.

APPROPRIATE GRADE LEVELS: 3–9

PERFORMANCE TIME: 3-1/2 minutes

THE NOVEL IN BRIEF: This is the second book in Sharon Jennings' Bats series. Sam and Simon (the Bat Gang) have to look after Sam's little sister on Halloween night. Soon the Bats end up in the graveyard – chased by a ghoul, crying for help. And then it all gets worse!

PERFORMING NOTES: The sound effects may be more important than any of the actors in this scene. Students will have to work carefully on timing to achieve a seamless performance. The two narrator roles are somewhat more difficult than those of Sam and Simon.

Narrator 1 (12 lines)
Narrator 2 (11 lines)
Sam (12 lines)
Simon (8 lines)

SOUND EFFECTS: *owl hooting, dog growling, dog barking, footsteps, thud, twig snapping, screams, evil laughing, spooky music*

Students may want to download some of these sound effects as MP3s, but getting playback timing right is very difficult.

<20 Bats in the Graveyard>

Bats in the Graveyard – Readers' Theater

Narrator 1
Narrator 2
Sam
Simon

SOUND EFFECTS: *owl hooting, dog growling, dog barking, footsteps, thud, twig snapping, screams, evil laughing, spooky music*

NARRATOR 1: This Readers' Theater play is adapted from the novel *Bats in the Graveyard* by Sharon Jennings. Today's actors are

_____

_____

_____

NARRATOR 2: Sam and Simon went to a graveyard to meet Fatso and his friends. They were scared, of course. But they had no choice.

NARRATOR 1: The two boys found some bushes in front of a big tombstone and sat down to wait.

SAM: What time is it, Simon?

SIMON: It's 9:42:05:43.

SAM: Couldn't you just say it's twenty to ten?

SIMON: I'm just telling you what my watch says.

SAM: So why hasn't Fatso shown up? What's that guy going to do? Just walk in the front gate and expect us to be scared?

NARRATOR 2: The two boys sat and waited. They heard an owl hooting. *(sound effect: owl hooting)* Then they heard a second owl hooting a little farther off. *(sound effect: owl hooting)*

SIMON: Those owls sound funny.

SAM: I don't think those are owls, Simon.

SIMON: You think it's Fatso?

SAM: Yeah, Fatso. *(pause)* And his friends.

SIMON: That means they're all out there . . . hiding. Maybe they've been watching us.

SAM: You know, we could just leave.

SIMON: No way. We either face up to them now or . . .

SAM: Or spend the rest of the year waiting for them to do something awful. *(sighs)* You're right. We'd better wait here.

(sound effect: owl hooting)

NARRATOR 1: After a while, the two boys stepped out from their hiding spot. They followed a path to the right. It led deeper and deeper into the graveyard. *(sound effect: footsteps)*

NARRATOR 2: As the path got farther and farther away from the street, the graveyard got darker and darker.

(sound effect: owl hooting)

SAM: Just keep walking, Simon. Don't look like you're afraid.

SIMON: What if I *am* afraid?

SAM: That's fine, *be* afraid. Just don't *look* afraid. Fatso could be watching.

NARRATOR 1:   So Sam and Simon kept going deeper into
the graveyard. Little paths kept branching off
from each other. Soon they were deep in the heart
of the graveyard . . . and lost.

NARRATOR 2:   Then they heard something that made their hearts
thump. A dog growled. *(sound effect: growl)*
Then the dog barked. *(sound effect: dog bark)*

NARRATOR 1:   It sounded as if the dog was about to jump on
them! *(sound effect: growling)*

SAM: Run!

SIMON: I'm way ahead of you! *(sound effect: running
footsteps)*

NARRATOR 2:   They ran and ran, twisting and turning
through the graveyard. The dog was always just
behind them. *(sound effect: growling)* The dog
kept growling as if he'd tear them apart.
(sound effect: growling)

NARRATOR 1:   And then, suddenly, the growling stopped.
Sam turned to look, but nothing was there.
Then he turned back to Simon.

NARRATOR 2:   But Simon wasn't there, either.

SAM: *(calling)* Simon. *(louder)* Simon! *(yelling)* SIMON!!

(sound effect: owl hooting)

NARRATOR 1:   Sam stood in the dark for a few minutes.
He was afraid to move in case Simon came back.
Then he heard a twig snap.
(sound effect: twig snapping)

NARRATOR 2:   Someone was out there.

SAM: Who's there? *(pause)* Simon? Is that you?

(sound effect: twig snaps again)

NARRATOR 1:   Then Sam remembered his flashlight. He
yanked it out of his pocket and shone it all around.
Then he wished he hadn't.

NARRATOR 2:   Only a few feet away, there was a ghoul, dripping
blood. The thing was huge! It towered over Sam.
And it was coming right toward him!

SAM: *(scream)*

NARRATOR 1:   Sam turned and ran. The ghoul followed him.
(sound effect: footsteps) Then Sam heard the dog
again. *(sound effect: growling)*

NARRATOR 2:   Sam didn't see the grave up ahead. He banged
into a tombstone and tripped. Then he fell
into a hole. *(sound effect: thud)*

NARRATOR 1:   From above, he heard laughing. It was crazy, evil
laughing. *(sound effect)*

NARRATOR 2:   Sam turned on his flashlight to see where
he had fallen. All around him, there was nothing
but earth. The hole was maybe two metres deep.
Make that six feet deep.

NARRATOR 1:   Six feet deep.

NARRATOR 1
and NARRATOR 2:   Sam had fallen into a grave!

(spooky music to close)

<The Crash 25>

The Crash

The school bus has just gone over a cliff. The bus driver is out cold. One of the guys on the basketball team is badly hurt. And then the bus catches on fire!

APPROPRIATE GRADE LEVELS: 4–8

PERFORMANCE TIME: 4 minutes

THE NOVEL IN BRIEF: A school bus is bringing a basketball team home after a game. Skidding on ice, the bus slides down a steep hill into deep snow. The bus driver is out cold. One of the guys is badly hurt. Craig, Rory and Lerch have to battle a snowstorm to find help.

PERFORMING NOTES: Craig's role is the most difficult of the three boys.' Both narrators, however, have more to read. Sound effects will greatly help the production.

Narrator 1 (10 lines)
Narrator 2 (10 lines)
Craig (14 lines)
Lerch (13 lines)
Rory (7 lines)

SOUND EFFECTS: *wind, door opening, explosion, grunting, coughing, jumping into snow, thumping*

<26 The Crash>

The Crash – Readers' Theater

Narrator 1
Narrator 2
Craig
Lerch
Rory

SOUND EFFECTS: *wind, door opening, explosion, grunting, coughing,*
jumping into snow, thumping

NARRATOR 1: This Readers' Theater play is adapted from the
novel *The Crash* by Paul Kropp. Today's actors are

_____

_____

_____

NARRATOR 2: The school bus has just gone over a cliff. Three of
the boys – Craig, Lerch and Rory – are not badly
hurt.

NARRATOR 1: But their friend Ben is badly hurt. Mrs. D, the bus
driver, is out cold.

NARRATOR 2: The bus is turned over on its side. Only the back
exit door will still open. And the boys can smell
leaking gas.

CRAIG: Okay, let's get Ben out first. I'll grab his arms
and you get his legs.

LERCH: Let's get moving. Smell that gas? This thing could
go up any minute.

CRAIG:	Rory, you get that seat belt off Mrs. D – she's next. And find that fire thing.
RORY:	The fire extinguisher?
CRAIG:	Yeah, find it – just in case.
NARRATOR 1:	Craig picked up Ben and dragged him. Because the bus was on its side, he had to pull him along the windows.
CRAIG:	*(grunting)* This guy is heavy. Lerch, can you give me some help?
LERCH:	I'll push, okay?
CRAIG:	Yeah, give it a try. *(grunting)*
NARRATOR 2:	All the pushing didn't help. Ben was still a dead weight, dragging along the windows.
CRAIG:	Forget it, I'll pull him by myself. You go help Rory with Mrs. D.
LERCH:	Okay.
NARRATOR 1:	So Craig pulled Ben to the back of the bus. He bit his lip and could taste blood. It was like metal, like iron, filling his mouth. But there was no time to stop and rest.
NARRATOR 2:	Craig pulled the red handle on the emergency door. *(sound effect: door opening)* The good news – it opened just fine. The bad news – there was a blizzard outside. *(sound effect – wind)*
RORY and LERCH:	Hey, you trying to freeze us out?
CRAIG:	Nah, I'm trying to *get* you out!
NARRATOR 1:	Craig jumped down into the snow. *(sound effect: thump)* Then he dragged Ben from the bus. *(sound effect: thump)*

NARRATOR 2: In the meantime, Lerch and Rory had dragged Mrs. D to the door.

LERCH: Here comes Mrs. D. *(sound effect: thump!)*

RORY: And I got the fire extinguisher. I'll bring it down with me.

NARRATOR 1: Lerch jumped down. *(sound effect: thump!)* Rory brought the fire extinguisher and Mrs. D's coat.

RORY: I've got to go back in.

CRAIG: You're nuts, Rory. That bus could go up in flames any second.

LERCH: Yeah, you can leave your math book, you jerk.

RORY: I need my coat, guys. I mean, it's cold out here.

LERCH: Hey, it's not worth it . . .

NARRATOR 2: But Rory didn't listen. He jumped up on the door, and then into the bus.

NARRATOR 1: Rory was only in the bus for ten seconds when the flames began. The fire was up front, under the motor. At first, the flames were small. But then . . .

LERCH: Rory! You've got to get out of there!

CRAIG: Move it, you jerk.

(sound effect: wind)

NARRATOR 2: Lerch was about to go in with the fire extinguisher when Craig grabbed him. He grabbed his legs and Lerch fell face first on the ground.

LERCH: What the . . .

NARRATOR 1: But Lerch didn't have time to finish.

(sound effect: explosion)

NARRATOR 2:   The whole front end of the bus went up in flames. Then the fire began moving toward the back.

LERCH and CRAIG: Rory! Get out of there!

NARRATOR 1:   The seats burst into flame, row by row.

LERCH: We've got to do something!

CRAIG: Don't go in there. You'll get killed!

NARRATOR 2:   Then the boys saw Rory at the back door of the bus. They heard him coughing *(sound effect: coughing)* – and then he jumped. *(sound effect: thump)* In a second, he was down on the snow.

CRAIG: You could have got killed, you jerk.

LERCH: You could have got *me* killed, too.

RORY: Yeah, but at least I got my coat. And it was plenty warm in there because of the fire.

CRAIG: You know, Rory. Sometimes I think you really are an idiot.

LERCH: So what do we do now, eh?

CRAIG: We wait. Somebody is going to find us.

RORY: Yeah, but Mrs. D is in bad shape. She might be bleeding inside. And Ben, he's bleeding outside.

LERCH: And it's getting cold, Craig. When the fire burns out, we're going to freeze.

NARRATOR 1:   Craig said nothing. He knew they were right. Things were bad.

NARRATOR 2:   And when the snow really came down, things were going to get worse.

(sound effect: wind, closing music)

Dark Ryder

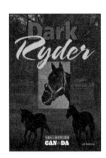

A spoiled girl, Victoria, is taking Dark Ryder over a set of jump fences when she falls to the ground. In anger, she offers to give the horse away – an offer that Kate accepts.

APPROPRIATE GRADE LEVELS: 4–9

PERFORMANCE TIME: 6 minutes

THE NOVEL IN BRIEF: A teenage girl, Kate, must somehow train a wild horse in order to keep him.

PERFORMING NOTES: This is the longest of our Readers' Theater plays. None of the character roles are particularly difficult, but the horse sound effects are quite essential to the story. The role of Doc Vickers is small and could be played by one of the narrators or the sound-effects person. The sound effect of horses' hooves can be made with plastic cups against a desk.

Narrator 1 (8 lines)
Narrator 2 (8 lines)
Kate – central character of the novel (13 lines)
Pat – a stable hand at the Peterson farm (10 lines)
Victoria – a spoiled teenage girl (13 lines)
Mr. Peterson – Victoria's father (10 lines)
Doc Vickers – a veterinarian (3 lines)

SOUND EFFECTS: *horse galloping, whipping sound, thump, girl crying, running steps, horse trotting, horse whinny*

<32 Dark Ryder>

Dark Ryder – Readers' Theater

Narrator 1
Narrator 2
Kate – central character of the story
Pat – a stable hand at the Peterson farm
Victoria – a spoiled teenage girl
Mr. Peterson – Victoria's father
Doc Vickers – a veterinarian

SOUND EFFECTS: *horse galloping, whipping sound, thump, girl crying, running steps, horse trotting, horse whinny*

NARRATOR 1: This Readers' Theater play is adapted from the novel *Dark Ryder* by Liz Brown. Today's actors are:

_____

_____

_____

NARRATOR 2: Kate walked over to the Peterson farm to try to get a summer job. She met up with her friend Pat, the stable hand.

PAT: Hey, Kate, what are you doing over here so early in the morning?

KATE: Hey, yourself. I came over to talk to Mr. Peterson about something.

PAT: Well, you're going to have a long wait. Mr. Peterson is busy telling Doc Vickers what a great rider the Princess is. He even brought in old Bart Myers to watch the kid ride.

<Dark Ryder 33>

NARRATOR 1: The two of them looked over to the ring where Victoria was riding. The teenage girl was trying to take Dark Ryder over a set of jump fences.

(sound effect in background: horse galloping)

VICTORIA: Watch this, Daddy!

MR. PETERSON: That's great, honey. *(to the men)* I told you my girl was quite the rider. Not every kid can handle a horse like Dark Ryder.

VICTORIA: Watch me do this one! *(sound effect: horse galloping)*

NARRATOR 2: Kate and Pat were not impressed.

KATE: I guess she's okay on the little jumps.

PAT: Too bad she has to whip Dark Ryder all the time. There are other ways to get a horse to jump.

KATE: Victoria likes to be in charge, you know. She'd whip you if she had the chance.

PAT: (laughing) Well, she is the Princess.

NARRATOR 1: Off in the training ring, Victoria was taking Dark Ryder to the taller gates.

MR. PETERSON: Be careful, honey.

VICTORIA: I can do these, Daddy. They're easy!

DOC VICKERS: Don't push that horse so hard, Victoria. He's going to balk at one of those gates.

VICTORIA: I'll make him do what I say, or he'll feel it. *(sound effect: whipping the horse)*

NARRATOR 2: Kate and Pat could only shake their heads.

KATE: Some of those jumps are really high.

<34 Dark Ryder>

PAT: They're from last night. Mr. Peterson brought some good riders out to the farm. But the Princess isn't stupid. She won't be trying those today. She's not ready.

NARRATOR 1: Almost as soon as Pat finished his words, Victoria aimed Dark Ryder at the highest jump. She was whipping the horse like crazy. *(sound effect: whipping sound, horse galloping)*

KATE: Looks like you spoke too soon, Pat.

PAT: I don't think Dark Ryder will take the jump. He's going to balk.

KATE: They're going for it.

PAT: I don't want to watch this.

NARRATOR 2: Dark Ryder pricked his ears forward. *(sound effect: galloping)* He built up speed, rushing to the fence, then took a powerful leap. He looked beautiful as he sailed over the fence. It was a perfect jump.

NARRATOR 1: But as the horse went up, Victoria lost her footing in the saddle. She struggled for control, then went flying into the air. In a second, Victoria landed on the ground. *(sound effect: thump, girl crying)*

NARRATOR 2: Everyone rushed out to see if she was all right. *(sound effect: running steps)*

MR. PETERSON: Vicky, Vicky!

VICTORIA: (crying)

DOC VICKERS: Don't move her! Just give her a little time.

MR. PETERSON: Are you all right, honey? Where does it hurt?

NARRATOR 1: Just then, Victoria rolled over and blinked away her tears.

VICTORIA:	Oh shut up, all of you!
MR. PETERSON:	Vicky, are you all right?
VICTORIA:	No, I'm *hurt*, Daddy. I hurt all over. And it's all the fault of that stupid horse.
NARRATOR 2:	Off to one side, Pat and Kate went to calm Dark Ryder.
PAT:	I guess the Princess isn't all that hurt.
KATE:	Guess not.
PAT:	Too bad she can't ride. That Dark Ryder is quite a horse.
KATE:	*(calling to the horse)* Here boy. *(to the horse)* It's all okay. It wasn't your fault.
NARRATOR 1:	Kate and Pat led Dark Ryder back to Victoria. *(sound effect: horse trotting)*
VICTORIA:	Get that stupid horse out of here. I never want to see him again!
MR. PETERSON:	Don't be like that, honey.
VICTORIA:	I'll be any way I want! I hate that horse!
MR. PETERSON:	Well, Doc, I don't know what we're going to do about this.
VICTORIA:	Daddy, I'm supposed to be riding at the Royal Winter Fair. I can't do it with that . . . thing! He's out of control! He could have killed me today!
MR. PETERSON:	I know how you feel, honey. Dark Ryder is a mean and nasty horse. Maybe we should just have him put down. What do you think Doc?
NARRATOR 2:	Before Doc Vickers could speak, Kate jumped in.
KATE:	No, you can't!

NARRATOR 1: The others turned to stare at her. Even her friend Pat was amazed.

KATE: You can't put him down. I'll . . . I'll buy him!
(sound effect: horse whinny)

PAT: You'll what?

KATE: I'll find the money and I'll buy him.

VICTORIA: But you don't have any money, Kate. Honestly, you and your gramps are just a cut up from trailer trash.

MR. PETERSON: Victoria, please.

VICTORIA: But it's true, Daddy. How is she going to afford a horse like this?

NARRATOR 2: All of them turned to look at Kate. It was true – Kate and her grandfather had very little money. Even boarding and feeding Dark Ryder would cost a lot. But Kate had an idea.

KATE: I'll work for you, Mr. Peterson – all summer. I'll be a stable hand, or anything, but I'll do it every day. That should be worth a few thousand dollars.

DOC VICKERS: Sounds like a fair deal to me, Jed. A second ago, you were going to put this horse down. Now Kate is offering you a deal. Shake hands on it. We can do the paperwork later.

VICTORIA: Do it, Daddy. I hate that horse. I never want to see Dark Ryder again.

KATE: Is it a deal, Mr. Peterson?

(pause)

MR. PETERSON: It's a deal, Kate. That damn horse is your problem now.

(closing music)

<Pump! 37>

Pump!

Pat and Ryan use some building supplies to create a skateboard ramp. All goes well until Pat's final test of the ramp.

APPROPRIATE GRADE LEVELS: 4–10

PERFORMANCE TIME: 5 minutes

THE NOVEL IN BRIEF: Pat is tired of being hassled by neighbors about his skateboarding. He wants a skateboard park so he can develop his skills. But getting that park built won't be easy.

PERFORMING NOTES: There should be a dedicated sound-effects person to handle the various sounds in the script.
Pat and Ryan are typical adolescents – excited at the prospect of building a skateboard ramp.
Mr. Perez is a kindly neighbor who helps the boys throughout the novel. His role is small and could be handled by Ryan if he added an accent or a deeper tone to his voice.

Narrator 1 (10 lines)
Narrator 2 (10 lines)
Pat (13 lines)
Ryan (9 lines)
Mr. Perez (4 lines)

SOUND EFFECTS: *skateboarding sounds, thunk, hammering and sawing, footsteps, knocking, pipes clanging, paper shuffling, scraping, siren, laugher, screaming mom*

<38 Pump!>

Pump! – Readers' Theater

Narrator 1
Narrator 2
Pat – a skateboarder
Ryan – Pat's friend
Mr. Perez – a neighbor

SOUND EFFECTS: *skateboarding sounds, thunk, hammering and sawing, footsteps, knocking, pipes clanging, paper shuffling, scraping, siren, laugher, screaming mom*

NARRATOR 1: This Readers' Theater play is adapted from the novel *Pump!* by Sharon Jennings. Today's actors are

_____

_____

_____

NARRATOR 2: Pat ran over to his friend Ryan's house. *(sound effect: footsteps)* Then he banged on the door. *(sound effect: knocking)*

PAT: Come on! Grab your wagon!

RYAN: What's going on, man?

PAT: There's a building site over on Elm Street. They've got wood and pipes and stuff. We've got to get over there and grab everything before someone else does.

RYAN: For what?

PAT: For a ramp, you idiot. Now let's move. *(sound effect: running steps)*

<Pump! 39>

NARRATOR 1: The two boys got to Elm Street in seconds.
They saw a pile of junk out on the curb
and hurried over.

NARRATOR 2: Pat grabbed a few pipes. *(sound effect: pipes clanging)* Ryan hauled out big sheets of wood. *(sound effect: wood clattering)* They were both excited.

RYAN: Oh, man! This is like finding treasure!
We can build a ramp just like we always wanted!

PAT: I've got some plans at home. It'll be easy.

Ryan: Sweet! Let's get started.

NARRATOR 1: The boys dumped everything in the shed behind Pat's house. *(sound effect: wood and pipes crashing)* Then they ran inside for a saw,
a hammer and nails. In no time, they were
ready to start.

RYAN: So, what kind are we going to build?

PAT: A vert ramp would be cool.

RYAN: Way cool. You ever done vert boarding?

PAT. Nah. But it'd be awesome.

RYAN: Absolutely awesome, man. Let's see those plans. *(sound effect: paper shuffling)*

NARRATOR 2: Making a vert ramp is trickier than it seems.
The boys hammered and sawed for hours. *(sound effects: hammering and sawing)*

NARRATOR 1: They were making so much noise that
old Mr. Perez looked over the fence at them.

MR. PEREZ: What are you kids building?

<40 Pump!>

PAT:	A ramp, Mr. Perez. *(whispering to Ryan)* Just what we need. I bet he's going to complain to my mom.
MR. PEREZ:	A ramp, eh? For skateboarding?
PAT:	Yeah. *(sound effect: hammering)*
MR. PEREZ:	My grandson made one of those ramps. You boys want a little advice?
PAT:	Well, maybe.
NARRATOR 2:	Soon Mr. Perez came over to help. He showed the boys how to fix the supports so their ramp wasn't lopsided. Then he showed them how to attach the pipes along the side of the ramp.
NARRATOR 1:	When all the work was done, Pat smiled at Mr. Perez and shook his hand.
PAT:	Thanks a lot, Mr. Perez. You want to try it out when we're done?
MR. PEREZ:	*(laughing)* I don't think my knees would like that. But I wouldn't mind watching you two. It seems like fun.
RYAN:	It *is* fun, Mr. Perez. It's the most fun there is!
NARRATOR 2:	Pat and Ryan finished the ramp just as it got dark. They hauled the ramp down the driveway and out to the street. *(sound effect: scraping)*
RYAN:	You go first, man.
PAT:	No problem. I'm ready.
NARRATOR 1:	Pat grabbed his board and manualed down the drive. *(sound effect: skateboarding)* Then he did a backside 180 off the ramp and he flew through the air.

NARRATOR 2:   He went about two metres before touching down. *(sound effect: thunk)*

PAT: Oh man! This is sweet! This is the best!

NARRATOR 1:   Then Ryan got on his board and did the same line. *(sound effect: skateboarding, then thunk)* Ryan pumped his fist in the air and laughed. *(sound effect: laughter)*

NARRATOR 2:   The boys went again and again, taking turns. They both fell a lot, especially when they tried grinding the pipes.

NARRATOR 1:   Then Pat decided to give it one more try. He went down the driveway, did a quick turn, went up the ramp and . . .

NARRATOR 2:   WHAM!

NARRATOR 1:   Pat smashed down on the pavement. Hard.

NARRATOR 2:   The next thing Pat knew, his mom was running down the sidewalk, screaming. *(sound effects: running, screaming mom)*

NARRATOR 1:   And a cop car was coming up the street. *(sound effect: siren)*

(closing music)

Caught in the Blizzard

Three teenagers are stranded in the Canadian Arctic. Their snowmobile is broken, the dog team is running back to town and a blizzard will soon be on them.

APPROPRIATE GRADE LEVELS: 5–12

PERFORMANCE TIME: 5 ½–6 minutes

THE NOVEL IN BRIEF: Three teenagers in the Arctic deal with personal rivalry and the issue of illegal poaching. Trapped on the land during a blizzard, all three discover new truths about themselves.

PERFORMING NOTES: Sam is a relatively quiet character. Connor spends much of his time either complaining or groaning. Both narrator roles are more difficult than those of the other actors.

Narrator 1 (11 lines)
Narrator 2 (11 lines)
Sam – an Inuk (15 lines)
Connor – a wealthy white teenager (15 lines)
Annie – a girl from Yellowknife (8 lines)

SOUND EFFECTS: *wind, barking dogs, a crash, groaning, wolf howling, cutting through snow*

Note that the pronunciation of komatik *(a snow sled) is ko' mah-tick (accent on the first syllable)*

<44 Caught in the Blizzard>

Caught in the Blizzard – Readers' Theater

Narrator 1
Narrator 2
Sam – an Inuk
Connor – a wealthy white teenager
Annie – a girl from Yellowknife

SOUND EFFECTS: *wind, barking dogs, a crash, groaning, wolf howling, cutting through snow*

NARRATOR 1: This Readers' Theater play is adapted from the novel *Caught in the Blizzard* by Paul Kropp.

NARRATOR 2: Today's actors are

_____

_____

_____

NARRATOR 1: At last, Sam and Annie found Connor lying on the snow. Connor's snowmobile was broken. Connor was shivering from the cold.

NARRATOR 2: Connor would have died if they had not found him. Still, he complained when they lifted him onto the dogsled.

(Sound effects: wind noise, dogs barking)

CONNOR: Can't your dogs go any faster? I'm freezing.

SAM: The dogs are tired. They do what they can.

CONNOR: Why didn't you bring a snowmobile? We could all freeze to death before we get to town on this thing.

<Caught in the Blizzard 45>

NARRATOR 1: The dogs barked as they pulled the sled. *(sound effect: barking)* The wind was blowing hard. *(sound effect: wind noise)*. It was driving snow into their faces.

ANNIE: Would you two just stop it. Connor, you really are a—

CONNOR: What did you call me?

NARRATOR 2: Connor turned back to look at Annie. His movement shifted the balance of the sled.

SAM: Don't do that . . .

NARRATOR 1: But it was already too late. Just as Connor turned, the *komatik* hit a rock hidden under the snow. The sled went flying into the air.

CONNOR: Wait . . .

SAM: Don't . . .

ANNIE: Oh no!

(sound effect: crash)

NARRATOR 2: Suddenly, the three of them went flying off the sled. Annie went sailing off first. Connor grabbed at Sam to hold on, but that only pulled Sam off, too.

NARRATOR 1: In seconds, the three of them were lying on the snow, groaning in pain *(sound effect: groaning)* Connor was in the worst shape.

CONNOR: My arm! *(screaming)* My arm!

ANNIE: You jerk! This is all your fault.

CONNOR: It wasn't me. It was Sam. He should have seen that rock. *(pause)* My arm — I swear it's broken twice.

<46 Caught in the Blizzard>

NARRATOR 2: Sam was a bit dazed at first. He felt as if he'd hit his head in the crash. But then the words between Annie and Connor became clear. It wasn't their fighting that bothered Sam. It was the missing *komatik.*

CONNOR: Where are those stupid dogs, Sam?

ANNIE: I can't see them anywhere.

SAM: They're gone. *(pause)*

(sound effect: wind whistling)

SAM: The snow anchor should have stopped the sled, but I guess it didn't work. Now the dogs will keep going right back to town.

ANNIE: You mean we're stuck out here?

CONNOR: How far do you expect me to walk with a broken arm?

SAM: We don't have to worry about walking. *(pause)* We've got to worry about staying alive.

*** *(interlude: music or wind sound effect)*

NARRATOR 1: Soon the blizzard was on them in full force. *(sound effect: wind)* The wind howled and the snow blew so hard that it stung their skin.

CONNOR: This is a stupid way to die. Stupid . . . stupid . . . stupid . . .

SAM: Listen, it'll be all right. My parents will call Search and Rescue if we're not back soon. But we'd better start building a shelter, just in case.

CONNOR: Build an igloo? With what? Our bare hands?

NARRATOR 2:   Sam's heart sank. There had been a snow knife on the dogsled. It had the perfect blade to carve the snow into blocks. But the *komatik* was racing back to town with the dogs.

CONNOR: So what do we do now, Sam? What's your next bright idea?

ANNIE: Hey, I've got a knife. *(pause)* I used to need it, down south. I was hanging with a rough crowd, you know?

NARRATOR 1:   The three of them fell silent as the wind howled. *(sound effect: wind)* The land spread before them, cold and flat. Sam searched the white snow and ice, trying to find someplace where they could build a shelter.

NARRATOR 2:   And there it was — a small hump covered with snow, just off to the right. It looked like a large pile of rocks, not quite as tall as a man. It would give them one wall for their shelter.

SAM: *(shouting)* Over there, come on!

ANNIE: What do we do?

SAM: We have to dig down into the snow. Here, away from the wind. We cut the snow with the knife and then pile up the blocks.

CONNOR: That's not a snow knife, you idiot. This will never work.

ANNIE: Shut up, Connor. *(pause)* Sam, I'll cut the blocks and you pile them up. *(sound effect: knife slicing into snow)*

SAM: Can you cut them bigger?

ANNIE: I'm doing the best I can. How deep do you want me to cut?

<48 Caught in the Blizzard>

SAM:	The deeper the better. Use two cuts, if you have to. Or here, Annie, you stack the blocks and I'll cut.
NARRATOR 1:	Annie agreed to the switch. Her arm was aching from trying to hack at the frozen snow. Her knife was half the size of what they needed.
NARRATOR 2:	The cutting and the building were slow jobs. The blocks had to be cut and stacked, one at a time. Finally Annie and Sam had dug down to the level of their knees. Their shelter was halfway built.
SAM:	You should get inside, Connor. You'll be warmer.
NARRATOR 1:	Connor grumbled but soon climbed into the hole in the snow. Quickly, Sam began cutting more blocks of snow. Annie kept building up the igloo, stacking the new blocks on top of the low walls.
NARRATOR 2:	The important thing was to cover the top, so they wouldn't lose heat through the night.

(sound effects: wind whistling)

CONNOR:	Are you trying to bury me?
SAM:	We're trying to keep you alive, Connor.
NARRATOR 1:	The wind was their greatest danger. The snow might bury them, but the wind could chill their bodies in just a few minutes.
SAM:	That will have to do it. Let's get inside.
NARRATOR 2:	The two of them climbed through the small opening of their igloo. Then they squeezed beside Connor.
CONNOR:	We're going to freeze to death and you've dug the grave yourself.

<Caught in the Blizzard 49>

SAM: We're not going to die, Connor. The igloo will hold the heat in and keep the storm out. If we had more food, we could last for a week like this. I think we can last till morning.

ANNIE: Morning? What if the blizzard doesn't let up?

SAM: Then the next day.

CONNOR: If the wolves don't get us. If we don't freeze to death first. If we don't starve or get buried under the snow.

NARRATOR 1: Neither Sam nor Annie wanted to hear any more. The makeshift igloo was good enough. It would keep them alive for one night, at least.

NARRATOR 2: After that the odds against them would get much, much worse.

(closing music or wind sound or wolf howling)

<Ghost House 51>

Ghost House

On a dare, three boys sneak into a haunted house to spend the night. Soon they're desperate to get out of the house, but they're trapped. And then a strange clock begins to chime.

APPROPRIATE GRADE LEVELS: 5–12

PERFORMANCE TIME: 5 minutes

THE NOVEL IN BRIEF: Three boys vow to spend an entire night in a haunted house, but the spooky noises and strange events are more than they bargained for.

PERFORMING NOTES: Tyler is relatively quiet and actually does believe in ghosts. Zach is a bit of a show-off and feels that ghosts are impossible. Hammy is a skateboarder and should be played with a bit of attitude. The real stars of this drama are the sound effects, which can be done by a single student or, with practice, by an entire class.

Narrator 1 (9 lines)
Narrator 2 (9 lines)
Tyler – the older brother (4 lines)
Zach – the younger brother (12 lines)
Hammy – a friend and a skateboarder (12 lines)

SOUND EFFECTS: *footsteps on stairs, thunder, wind, wood hitting glass, grunting, heavy breathing, the bells (clock chime: "dong"), branches tapping glass*

<52 Ghost House>

Ghost House – Readers' Theater

Narrator 1
Narrator 2
Tyler – the older brother
Zach – the younger brother
Hammy – a friend

SOUND EFFECTS: *footsteps on stairs, thunder, wind, wood hitting glass, grunting, heavy breathing, the bells (clock chime: "bong"), branches tapping glass*

NARRATOR 1: This Readers' Theater play is adapted from the novel *Ghost House* by Paul Kropp. Today's actors are

_____

_____

_____

NARRATOR 2: The three boys stood in the dark room, staring at the plywood on the window. Hammy was shaking his head. Tyler was feeling a little creepy. And Zach was angry.

ZACH: If Alex nailed that plywood back on, I'm going to kill him.

HAMMY: Not a good idea. Look what happened to the guy in the paper.

ZACH: Yeah, right. So I'll just cause him terrible pain and suffering. Maybe I'll tell Tasha that he's got the hots for her. *(all three boys laugh)*

NARRATOR 1: Zach and Hammy still seemed pretty cool, despite what had gone on . . .

<Ghost House 53>

NARRATOR 2: But Tyler was scared. He tried hard to hide it from the others, but inside he was shaking. Everything had been just too weird. Now the three boys were stuck in the Blackwood house for the whole night.

ZACH: I've got an idea. It sounds like some of those branches are blowing up against the house. *(sound effect: branches tapping window)* All we have to do is open one of the upstairs windows. Then we just climb down a tree.

TYLER: I don't think . . .

ZACH: Come on, Tyler. We've been stuck in here long enough. Let's go.

NARRATOR 1: The three boys made their way upstairs. (*sound effect: footsteps*) Getting up the stairs was no big deal. Every so often there was a flash of lightning so the boys could see their way.

NARRATOR 2: Zach got to the top first, followed by the others. Nobody said much. All they could think about was getting out of the house.

NARRATOR 1: Upstairs, there was a little more light. The storm was back in full force. Thunder rattled the doors and windows. *(sound effect: thunder)*

NARRATOR 2: Lightning flashed across the night sky. The wind outside was like a hurricane. *(sound effect: wind)*

HAMMY: It sure is dark.

ZACH: With a storm like this, I bet the lights are out all over town.

HAMMY: Let's see if we can open the window at the end of the hall. *(sound effect: footsteps)*

ZACH: I'm on it.

<54 Ghost House>

HAMMY: Push on your side . . .

NARRATOR 1: Zach pushed up on the right side, Hammy on the left. *(sound effect: grunting)* But the window didn't budge.

HAMMY: The window must be painted shut.

ZACH: Or maybe the house has shifted. I bet nobody has tried to open a window here for thirty years.

NARRATOR 2: Tyler said nothing. Some part of him knew that the window wouldn't open. Some part of him knew that none of the windows would open.

ZACH: This is stupid! These windows are stuck tight.

HAMMY: We could smash one. *(sound effect: thunder)*

NARRATOR 1: The thunder came like an answer.

ZACH: Somebody might hear and call the cops, but at least we'd be out of this place. I wish there was some other way.

NARRATOR 2: He had just finished talking when the sound came:

BONG!

HAMMY: What the . . . ?

TYLER: It's a bell. It sounds like the chime of a big old clock.

BONG!

ZACH: So how could there be a clock in this old place? And how come we didn't hear it before?

BONG!

HAMMY: I don't know about you guys, but I say we smash a window and get out of here.

BONG!

NARRATOR 1: Quickly, Zach picked up a hunk of wood from the floor. He smashed it against the window. *(sound effect: hitting glass)*

BONG!

TYLER: Hey, the glass didn't break.

HAMMY: Here, let me try it.

NARRATOR 2: Hammy took the piece of wood and smashed it into the glass. *(sound effect: hitting glass)*

BONG!

NARRATOR 1: The glass might as well have been steel.

HAMMY: Here, Tyler, you try it!

BONG!

NARRATOR 2: Tyler was the oldest and the strongest, but he knew it was useless. Still, he took the wood from Hammy.

BONG!

NARRATOR 1: Tyler swung the wood against the glass once *(sound effect)*, twice *(sound effect)*, three times *(sound effect)*.

BONG!

NARRATOR 1: The glass didn't even shake. Zach grabbed the wood from his brother and threw it at the window. *(sound effect: hitting glass)*

BONG!

ZACH: This is so stupid!

HAMMY: This is, like, really strange.

BONG!

<56 Ghost House>

NARRATOR 2: Suddenly it was quiet. The storm died down and the bell stopped ringing. The only sound the boys could hear was their own breathing. *(sound effect: heavy breathing)*

TYLER: Eleven o'clock. It's that time – the time of the murder.

HAMMY: And we're trapped. We can't get out.

ZACH: *(high, frightened voice)* I don't like this . . . I don't like this at all.

(ominous closing music)

<One Crazy Night 57>

One Crazy Night

In one wild night at a small country store, everything goes wrong all at once.

APPROPRIATE GRADE LEVELS: 6–10

PERFORMANCE TIME: 5 minutes

THE NOVEL IN BRIEF: The novel tells the story of the adventures and misadventures of Todd, a typical teenager, while working at a small-town delicatessan and gas station. One stormy night, Todd has to deal with a woman going into labor, an attempted robbery and even worse, the meanest grade 5 teacher ever.

PERFORMING NOTES: Todd is the "straight" man in this scene. Elaine should sound like an airhead. Mrs. Plotnik is mean and cranky, and quite sarcastic in many of her lines. The Punk is actually less dangerous and more sympathetic than he appears here. This play works very well with a wide range of students. Good actors, especially, will have fun hamming up their roles.

Narrator 1 (9 lines)
Narrator 2 (9 lines)
Todd – a teenager employed at the variety store
(9 lines)
Elaine – a pregnant young woman (11 lines)
Mrs. Plotnik – a cranky grade 5 teacher (6 lines)
The Punk – appears to be a tough guy (10 lines)

SOUND EFFECTS: *rain, thunder, dripping, cell phone ring (*Gilligan's Island *theme), smash, footsteps*

<58 One Crazy Night>

One Crazy Night – Readers' Theater

Narrator 1
Narrator 2
Todd – a teenager employed at the variety store
Elaine – a pregnant young woman
Mrs. Plotnik – a cranky grade 5 teacher
The Punk – appears to be a tough guy

SOUND EFFECTS: *rain, thunder, dripping, cell phone ring (*Gilligan's Island *theme), smash, footsteps*

NARRATOR 1: This Readers' Theater play is adapted from *One Crazy Night* by Paul Kropp. Today's actors are

_____

_____

_____

NARRATOR 2: There were four people inside the small store. The weather outside was so bad that no one wanted to leave.

(sound effect: rain, thunder)

NARRATOR 1: Even inside the store, it wasn't all that nice. There was water dripping down the back wall. More water was dripping from the roof. *(sound effect: dripping water)*

NARRATOR 2: The punk went over to the DVD rack as if he were going to check one out. *(sound effect: footsteps).* Actually, he was looking at the cash register.

ELAINE: You know, Todd, this is a little scary. I bet it's flooded under the Main Street Bridge. I mean, if I go into labor tonight, how do I get to the hospital?

<One Crazy Night 59>

TODD:	Oh, I could drive you on some back roads.
MRS. PLOTNIK:	I wouldn't trust this young man to drive you anywhere. Not after what he did to my classroom six years ago.
TODD:	That was an accident, Mrs. Plotnick.
NARRATOR 1:	Todd did not want to think about grade 5. Mrs. Plotnik had been his teacher. That was the year he flooded her classroom.
NARRATOR 2:	Actually, that was the year he flooded the whole school!
MRS. PLOTNIK:	There are no accidents, Todd. Only idiots.
ELAINE:	Oh, Mrs. Plotnik, there are many accidents. I mean, look at me. Jimmy and I would never have planned for a baby right now, right when he's off to prison. *(pause)* But here's our baby!
TODD:	Jimmy? Jimmy who?
ELAINE:	Well, Jimmy Branson, of course.
TODD:	You mean Jimmy Branson is your husband? How could you marry a goofball like that?
ELAINE:	Oh, Jimmy seemed so full of fun and so kind when I met him. He kept telling me that I was the sweetest girl he'd ever met.
NARRATOR 1:	Jimmy used the same line on every girl from grade 5 on.
ELAINE:	So we snuck off and got married. And now, well, you see what happened.
MRS. PLOTNIK:	I repeat – no accidents, only idiots.
ELAINE:	Oh, Jimmy isn't an idiot. I'm sure when he gets out of prison, he'll be a very good father.

NARRATOR 2:	Suddenly Todd's phone began to ring. *(sound effect: Ta-dum-ta-dum-ta-ta-ta-dum . . .)* It was his mother.
TODD:	I'm fine, mom. There's no power but I'm fine. (pause) Yes, I loved the soup. I always love your soup, mom.
NARRATOR 1:	The rain poured down outside. *(sound effect: rain)* There was a crash of thunder. *(sound effect: thunder)* Then the punk shouted from the back of the store.
PUNK:	Hey, you. You work here?
TODD:	Yeah, I'm the entire night staff. I'm vice president of sandwiches. CEO of the pop machine.
PUNK:	Pretty funny guy. *(pause)* Listen, I need some money and some smokes.
TODD:	Well, the cash register won't work without power. But if you have the exact change, I can sell you a package of smokes.
PUNK:	Who says I'm *buying?*
NARRATOR 2:	The punk reached into his jacket pocket.
PUNK:	This is a holdup!
ELAINE:	A holdup?
MRS. PLOTNIK:	A holdup? A punk like you thinks he can do a holdup? Where's your getaway car?
PUNK:	Uh . . . around the corner.
ELAINE:	You don't really want to do a holdup. I mean, armed robbery is a very bad thing. You could get four to ten years in prison. For what? If Jimmy were here, he'd tell you it's not worth it. Prison is no fun.

<One Crazy Night 61>

NARRATOR 1: The punk seemed to be thinking about all this. If Elaine had been able to keep going, she might have talked him out of the robbery. But then Mrs. Plotnik spoke up.

MRS. PLOTNIK: You're just as stupid as Todd.

PUNK: Who are you calling stupid?

MRS. PLOTNIK: You, child. If you'd taken math from me, you'd be able to figure it out. Five cartons of cigarettes for five years in prison. That's 5000 cigarettes for 1500 days out of your life. So you're saying that your life is worth roughly three smokes a day. *(pause)* I don't think you value yourself very highly.

NARRATOR 2: The punk was confused by Mrs. Plotnik's math. Finally, he gave up trying to figure it out.

PUNK: Oh, shut up. *(to Todd)* You there, pimple-nose, get me a box. I'm taking all the smokes you got.

ELAINE: Oh, you'll regret this. Each day in prison, my Jimmy regrets what he did.

TODD: What did Jimmy do?

ELAINE: He borrowed a car.

TODD: It must have been a pretty nice car.

ELAINE: Actually, it was a police car. It was a silly thing to do, really, but he wanted to see how the siren worked.

NARRATOR 1: Suddenly Todd's phone rang. *(sound effect: Ta-dum-ta-dum-ta-ta-ta-dum . . .)*

PUNK: Ain't that the theme from *Gilligan's Island*? Man, you really should get a decent ring tone.

NARRATOR 2: Todd's phone rang again. *(sound effect: Ta-dum-ta-dum-ta-ta-ta-dum . . .)*

<62 One Crazy Night>

PUNK: I can't stand that ring tone! Give me that phone!

NARRATOR 1: The punk threw Todd's phone to the floor. It smashed. *(sound effect: smash)*

NARRATOR 2: Outside, the rain kept falling. *(sound effect: rain)* Inside, things were bad . . . and then they got worse.

NARRATOR 1: Coming toward the store was a moving light. It kept getting closer, coming toward the door.

NARRATOR 2: The punk was getting scared.

PUNK: You, pimple-nose, get back behind the counter. The rest of you, stay cool. If you all keep quiet, nobody will get hurt.

(closing music)

<Against All Odds 63>

Against All Odds

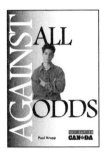

Three teenagers are trapped in an underground storm sewer. A thunderstorm rages above them. The boys are desperate to escape. As the water rises around them, they learn that one of them doesn't know how to swim.

APPROPRIATE GRADE LEVELS: 6–12

PERFORMANCE TIME: 4 minutes

NOTE: *This gritty scene should not be used with sensitive students.*

THE NOVEL IN BRIEF: A special student risks his life in the storm sewers beneath the city to gain respect from his older brother.

PERFORMING NOTES: Larry does most of the serious acting. Jeff's role is the easiest. Sound effects are important but can be done by the student actors, if necessary.

Narrator 1 (7 lines)
Narrator 2 (8 lines)
Larry – the older brother (12 lines)
Jeff – the younger brother, a special student at school (6 lines)
Tank – Jeff's friend, a bully (8 lines)

SOUND EFFECTS: *clanging metal, rushing water, pounding, climbing steps, car on a wet street*

The boys are in a sewer tunnel, so any echo effect will add to the sense of reality.

<64 Against All Odds>

Against All Odds – Readers' Theater

Narrator 1
Narrator 2
Larry – the older brother
Jeff – the younger brother
Tank – Jeff's friend, a bully

SOUND EFFECTS: *clanging metal, rushing water, pounding, climbing steps, car on a wet street*

NARRATOR 1: This Readers' Theater play is adapted from *Against All Odds* by Paul Kropp. Today's actors are

_____

_____

_____

NARRATOR 2: The three boys were trapped in the storm sewer. They were knee deep in cold water and very scared.

NARRATOR 1: Over their heads, on the surface, a terrible storm was raging. The rainstorm was sending torrents of water into the sewer.

NARRATOR 2: With each minute, the water in the tunnel was getting higher.

TANK: So did you bring help?

LARRY: Help?

TANK: Yeah, you brought somebody down with you, right?

NARRATOR 1: There was a moment of silence. Larry *was* "the help." And he had no idea what to do. His little brother, Jeff, didn't know this.

<Against All Odds 65>

JEFF: I told you Larry would save us.

LARRY: Yeah, right. I . . . uh . . . well. My girlfriend is calling the police.

NARRATOR 2: Tank got angry.

TANK: So you just came down here by yourself? How dumb are you? You can't play hero without some kind of plan.

LARRY: Well, I guess I didn't think. Do you guys know where we are?

TANK: *(sarcastic)* Beats me, Larry. I was looking for a street sign but its kind of dark down here. You didn't happen to bring a flashlight with you, or maybe a cell phone? I mean, that would have called for a little brainpower.

NARRATOR 1: Larry was upset. He had rushed into the sewer to save his brother. He didn't have a plan. He didn't know how to get out. All he knew was that Jeff was in trouble.

JEFF: Larry's got a light on his keychain.

LARRY: Yeah, let's see what's up there.

NARRATOR 2: Larry turned on the flashlight. He shone the light over the concrete walls. Then, up above, he saw a shaft that led to the surface.

LARRY: What's up there?

TANK: It must be where the side sewer connects to the main line. That's a manhole cover up at the top of the shaft.

LARRY: So why don't we just climb out?

JEFF: Because the manhole cover is locked.

<66 Against All Odds>

LARRY: Locked?

TANK: The city locked it down 'cause one day we kind of pushed it off.

NARRATOR 1: For a moment, there was silence. The only sound was water rushing through the sewer. That's when Larry had an idea.

LARRY: Jeff, give me your belt.

JEFF: My belt?

LARRY: Just take it off and give it to me. I'm going up to make some noise.

NARRATOR 2: In a second, Larry was climbing up the ladder. *(sound effect: footsteps)* Jeff kept the flashlight aimed on the rungs. When Larry reached the top, he pushed on the manhole cover. *(sound effect: grunting)*

NARRATOR 1: The manhole cover didn't budge.

NARRATOR 2: Then he began pounding on the metal, yelling for help.

LARRY: Hey, we're down here! *(sound effect: pounding)* Help! *(sound effect: pounding)* We need some help down here!

NARRATOR 1: Then Larry heard a sound over his head. *(sound effect: car splashing water)* It was a car running over the manhole cover.

LARRY: Oh, no! We're in the middle of the street! Nobody can hear us up there! It's hopeless!

NARRATOR 2: Larry climbed back down the ladder. *(sound effect: footsteps)* By now, the water had gone up another two inches.

LARRY: Can we get out that side tunnel?

<Against All Odds 67>

TANK: Too slippery.

LARRY: What about the big tunnel up ahead?

JEFF: It goes way down to the river.

NARRATOR 1: In front of them was the main line of the storm sewer. The water in the big tunnel was rushing by like a real river. It was swirling and bubbling, with dirt and branches floating on the surface.

LARRY: So how about we go with the flow? Jeff's a good swimmer and there's enough air at the top of the tunnel. If we wait, the water will fill this whole place and we'll never make it.

JEFF: Hey, that's smart, Larry.

NARRATOR 2: The two brothers looked at Tank in the darkness. He was shaking his head.

LARRY: I think it's the best plan.

TANK: Yeah, maybe for you guys. But I can't swim.

(sound effect: rushing water)

(closing music)

<Avalanche 69>

Avalanche

A group of students has gone to the mountains of British Columbia for a winter camping trip. Conditions are ripe for an avalanche, but no one expects danger at this point in the story.

APPROPRIATE GRADE LEVELS: 6–12

PERFORMANCE TIME: 5 minutes

THE NOVEL IN BRIEF: A group of teens is trapped by an avalanche in British Columbia – not all of them survive. Based on a true story.

PERFORMING NOTES: Tom is a light-hearted joker, Noah more serious. The two narrator roles are somewhat more difficult than the character roles because they involve longer blocks of text. Note that this chapter precedes the avalanche in the novel. There should be a general tone of gloom and foreboding. Sound effects are relatively unimportant.

Narrator 1 (7 lines)
Narrator 2 (6 lines)
Noah – reluctant to join on the trip, friend of Tom (14 lines)
Tom – athletic teenager, friend of Noah (5 lines)
Mike – a show-off and a bully (2 lines)
Brooke – a teenage girl (9 lines)
Mrs. Falletta – teacher supervisor (3 lines)

(The roles of Brooke and Mrs. Falletta can be done by one actor. The role of Mike can be added to Tom's role.)

SOUND EFFECTS: *rifle shots (best done with a clap or by hitting a ruler against the desk), wind noise*

<70 Avalanche>

Avalanche – Readers' Theater

Narrator 1
Narrator 2
Tom – athletic teenager, friend of Noah
Noah – reluctant to join the trip, friend of Tom
Mike – a show off and bully
Brooke – a teenage girl
Mrs. Falletta – teacher supervisor

SOUND EFFECTS: *rifle shots, wind noise*

NARRATOR 1: This Readers' Theater play is adapted from
Avalanche by Paul Kropp. Today's actors are

_____

_____

_____

NARRATOR 2: There were fifteen students and five adults on
the mountain that day. Early in the morning, the
group got ready for a day of cross-country skiing.
They needed a full day to reach the Arctic huts
for camping that night.

NARRATOR 1: Tom and Noah were talking as the day began.

NOAH: *(taking a deep breath)* So this is mountain air.

TOM: Hey, it's good for you. This whole thing is going
to build your character.

NOAH: I've already got character.

TOM: So after this you'll have more. You can't have
too much character, you know. You can even loan
some to me if you can't handle it all.

NARRATOR 2:   Then they heard the voice of Mrs. Falletta shouting to the group.

MRS. FALLETTA: Okay, kids, we've got a little over 10 K to cover before lunch. Then you'll get some hot food . . . unless I hear a lot of complaining. If you whine about the cold, all you get is a baloney sandwich.

(sound effect: kids laughing)

NARRATOR 1:   In the distance, the kids could hear some loud rifle shots.

(sound effect: three shots)

MIKE: Hey, what was that?

MRS. FALLETTA: Relax. The ski patrol is just shooting some of the snow up on the ridge. They knock it down to prevent avalanches.

MIKE: Yeah, but what if we're under the snow when they shoot?

MRS. FALLETTA: Then we won't have to listen to any more of your questions, Mike. *(sound effect: kids laughing)*

NOAH: Hey, Tom, remind me why I signed up for this.

TOM: Because you love skiing and the snow and the mountains.

NOAH: You've got to be kidding.

TOM: Okay, it's because you've got the hots for Brooke Ashton, that's why. This gives you an excuse to be near her.

NOAH: Hey, would you stop that.

(sound effect: more gun shots)

<72 Avalanche>

NARRATOR 2: The group set out across the mountain. By ten, the morning mist had cleared. The sun beamed down on the students, warming them. They had put on one layer too many, and now were hot from the work of skiing.

NARRATOR 1: By lunch, all the kids were starving. Mrs. Falletta cooked hamburgers on a tiny stove and made some hot cocoa to wash them down. The group had skied for three hours and covered 10 K. So far, the biggest danger they faced was sunburn.

NARRATOR 2: But mountain weather can't be trusted. After lunch, clouds began to roll in. The air got damp and the wind got worse. *(sound effect: wind)* And then came the snow.

NOAH: I can't believe this. It was perfect just an hour ago.

TOM: Believe it. I have a hunch this snow will get worse before we're done.

NOAH: It's the wind that makes it so bad. *(sound effect: wind)*

NARRATOR 1: The skiers could hardly see each other in the storm. Still, they kept going. The Arctic huts could not be much farther.

NARRATOR 2: Noah could hardly see. His goggles were all fogged up.

NARRATOR 1: Suddenly, Noah tripped over something on the path. He lost his balance, tipped to the left, and fell. Only then could he see what made him fall.

NARRATOR 2: It was Brooke Ashton, lying on the snow.

BROOKE: *(crying)*

<Avalanche 73>

NOAH:　Brooke, are you all right?

BROOKE:　Everything hurts. Everything! *(sniffling)*

NOAH:　Just rest for a while. I'll stay with you until you're ready to go on.

BROOKE:　Thanks, Noah.

NOAH:　It's lousy trying to ski in this weather. Tomorrow we get to use snowshoes. That should be more fun.

BROOKE:　You think so?

NOAH:　Yeah, I think so. You feeling any better?

BROOKE:　A little. Can you help me up?

NARRATOR 1:　With Noah's help, Brooke got back on her skis. By now, they were the last skiers in the group.

BROOKE:　Will you stay with me and make sure I'm okay?

NOAH:　Sure. It's not that much farther to the camp.

BROOKE:　Well, I think I can make it.

NOAH:　I'll be here if you get into trouble.

BROOKE:　You know, something about this whole trip is giving me a bad feeling. The storm is like an omen, you know?

NOAH:　I don't believe in omens. All we have to do is be careful and everything will be fine. After this storm, I bet everything will be just great.

BROOKE:　I hope so. I just hope so.

(ominous closing music)

<Scarface 75>

Scarface

Beamis and his racist buddies come to the video store owned by Tranh's uncle. For a laugh, they make fun of Tranh and vandalize the store.

APPROPRIATE GRADE LEVELS: 6–10

PERFORMANCE TIME: 5-1/2 minutes

THE NOVEL IN BRIEF: A recent immigrant deals with racism and bullying at school but learns on a ski trip that the rich boy who picks on him has his own set of problems.

PERFORMING NOTES: Both narrators have more to read than any of the other characters, but their roles are otherwise simple. The character of Beamis is the most difficult to portray. Tranh is quiet and speaks in a monotone through most of the play. Jeff and Randy are very minor characters. The sound effects are of little importance but add to the general ambience.

Note that Beamis sometimes utters racist remarks. Remind the audience that the student actor is representing a character in a novel, not his own feelings.

Narrator 1 (9 lines)
Narrator 2 (9 lines)
Tranh – a recent immigrant from Cambodia (13 lines)
Tranh's uncle – owns the video store (5 lines)
Beamis – a racist bully (12 lines)
Jeff – Beamis' football buddy (7 lines)
Randy – another football player (5 lines)

SOUND EFFECTS: *cash register, door opening, door slamming, DVDs falling to the floor, laughter, shouts*

<76 Scarface>

Scarface – Readers' Theater

Narrator 1
Narrator 2
Tranh – a recent immigrant from Cambodia
Tranh's Uncle – owns the video store
Beamis – a racist bully
Jeff – Beamis' football buddy
Randy – another football player

SOUND EFFECTS: *cash register, door opening, door slamming, DVDs falling to the floor, laughter, shouts*

NARRATOR 1: This Readers' Theater play is adapted from *Scarface* by Paul Kropp.

NARRATOR 2: Today's actors are

_____

_____

_____

NARRATOR 1: Tranh worked at his uncle's video store. His uncle's name was Tranh, too, but he called his store Mountain Video and DVD.

NARRATOR 2: Tranh felt lucky to be in Canada and to have a job. His uncle had sponsored him and made it possible to come here. He had given him a place to live with his own family. Now he treated Tranh like a son.

NARRATOR 1: Work at the video store was usually quiet. But one night . . .

(sound effect: cash register)

<Scarface 77>

UNCLE: Tranh, can you look after the store while I go home? My niece is sick with some kind of flu. I'll be back in an hour or two.

TRANH: Don't worry. Tuesday is always a slow night. I'll be fine on my own.

UNCLE: All the stock is back on the shelves, the computer is working well. If there is any problem –

TRANH: I can handle it. No problem.

(sound effect: door slamming)

NARRATOR 2: Tranh liked these English phrases, the ones he did not learn in the camp. *No problem. Sure thing. Piece of cake, eh?* When he used them, he felt as if he belonged here. It was as if he had finally found a home.

(sound effect: door slamming, laughter and shouts from the gang)

NARRATOR 1: Tranh was alone, in the back of the store, when the gang came in. He didn't notice them at first. Then he heard Beamis's voice and turned to look.

BEAMIS: Well, look who's here! *(laughter from the gang)*

NARRATOR 2: Tranh said nothing. His uncle always told him that the customer is king in this new country. His uncle had said, "the customer is always right." Tranh tried hard to believe that.

JEFF: Hey, look, it's Train Tracks! *(more laughter)*

RANDY: *(sarcastic)* Oooh. Better watch it, or Train Tracks will report us to the vice-principal.

BEAMIS: Nah, we can call him anything we want here. There's nothing Watson can do to us outside school hours. Right, *Scarface?*

<78 Scarface>

OTHER BOYS:	Ooooh!
NARRATOR 2:	Tranh turned his head so the gang could only see the left side of his face, the good side. He kept his eyes down, trying to keep the anger inside.
JEFF:	Okay, I'm bored. Let's get a DVD and get out of here.
NARRATOR 1:	Tranh saw Beamis and his friends walk to the "adult" part of the store. They were looking at boxes of X-rated videos and DVDs.
JEFF, BEAMIS, RANDY:	Whoo, look at this. Wow. Ever see something like that? Oh, I love that! *(Etc.)*
RANDY:	Hey, Tranh, you ever watch these movies?
TRANH:	No.
NARRATOR 2:	That was the truth. His uncle said those videos show no respect to women, or to men either. Still, the store had to stock them. Business was business.
JEFF:	How about we check out this one?
TRANH:	You must be eighteen.
BEAMIS:	Suppose I tell you I *am* eighteen.
TRANH:	I know you are not.
BEAMIS:	Scarface, I wonder how someone as dumb as you ever got into this country.
NARRATOR 1:	Tranh stared at Beamis but said nothing. His hands were trembling – not from fear, but from anger.
JEFF:	So you won't let us take out any of these?

NARRATOR 2: Beamis ran his hand along one shelf and knocked down all the boxes. *(sound effect: boxes smashing to the floor)* The other boys laughed. *(sound effect: laughter)*

TRANH: They are not for you.

RANDY: Or these? *(sound effect: boxes smashing on floor)*

TRANH: I think you should leave the store. We do not need your business.

BEAMIS: And I think you do. You know, my father could buy and sell this place in two seconds flat. You'd be out on your duff so fast you wouldn't even know what happened.

TRANH: This is my uncle's store. He does not want to sell.

BEAMIS: *(sarcastic)* Well isn't that nice. I guess these gooks are doing okay, aren't they?

JEFF: Taking over the whole country.

RANDY: Taking all the decent jobs.

BEAMIS: Even giving jobs to somebody like Scarface here. It's like hiring the handicapped. *(sound effect: laughter)*

TRANH: I think it is time for all of you to leave.

BEAMIS: After we get a movie or two.

NARRATOR 1: Quickly, Beamis stepped around the counter and pulled a DVD from the shelf behind Tranh's head.

BEAMIS: Here, guys, I got the one we wanted.

TRANH: That's on hold. You can't just –

NARRATOR 2: Tranh reached out and grabbed Beamis's arm. Beamis tried to pull free, but Tranh's grip was too strong. Beamis was surprised at the sudden pain in his wrist.

BEAMIS: Hey, gook, if you won't let go . . .

NARRATOR 1: Suddenly, the door opened. *(sound effect: door opening)* Standing there was Tranh's uncle. He looked at the boxes on the floor, then at Beamis behind the counter, then at Tranh.

UNCLE: What's going on?

BEAMIS: Uh, nothing.

JEFF: That's right. Just a little disagreement. Looks like your guy here doesn't want our business.

NARRATOR 2: Tranh's uncle looked at the gang. He did not know what to say. But he could see the big blond kid and his friends heading to the door.

BEAMIS: See you in school . . . Scarface. *(sound effect: door slamming)*

UNCLE: These are your friends?

TRANH: Not friends, Uncle, but I know them from school.

UNCLE: Sometimes I wonder what they teach in schools that boys learn to hate like that.

TRANH: The schools don't teach them to hate. But they cannot stop them from being stupid.

(closing music)

<Three Feet Under 81>

Three Feet Under

Scott and Rico have gone into an old mine to search for long-buried treasure, but they find that the school bully has reached it before them.

APPROPRIATE GRADE LEVELS: 6–10

PERFORMANCE TIME: 3-1/2 minutes

THE NOVEL IN BRIEF: Scott and Rico find a map to long-lost treasure – $250,000 buried in Bolton's mine. But when the school bully steals their map and heads for the old mine, the race to find the treasure is on.

PERFORMING NOTES: Sound effects are essential to make this Readers' Theater play work, and they should be assigned to a student who does not have a speaking role. Pacing is the most important aspect of performance. This short play is about confrontation and physical danger, so the timing must be tight for the play to be effective.

Narrator 1 (10 lines)
Narrator 2 (10 lines)
Scott – one of the heroes, an eleven-year-old (3 lines)
Rico – the other hero; Scott's friend (7 lines) (pronounced "Ree-koh")
Clay – the villain, a teenage bully (7 lines)

SOUND EFFECTS: *Footsteps, creaking, crashing, clang, collapsing mine*

<82 Three Feet Under>

Three Feet Under – Readers' Theater

Narrator 1
Narrator 2
Scott – one of the heroes, an eleven-year-old
Rico – the other hero, Scott's friend
Clay – the villain, a teenage bully

SOUND EFFECTS: *footsteps, creaking, crashing, clang, collapsing mine*

NARRATOR 1: This Readers' Theater play is adapted from *Three Feet Under* by Paul Kropp. Today's actors are

_____

_____

_____

NARRATOR 2: Scott and Rico reached the end of the tunnel. In front of them was Clay. He was digging into the mine floor.

NARRATOR 1: The two boys watched from the darkness.

(sound effect: digging, then hitting metal)

CLAY: *(talking to himself)* Got it!

NARRATOR 2: Clay lifted an old metal box from the ground. He took the shovel and smashed open the lid.

(sound effect: clang)

NARRATOR 1: Clay opened the box and looked inside.

(sound effect: creak)

CLAY: Well, look at that! Looks like I hit the jackpot!

<Three Feet Under 83>

NARRATOR 2:   Clay scooped out handfuls of money. He was laughing to himself. *(sound effect: laughing)*

NARRATOR 1:   That's when Scott yelled out from the darkness.

SCOTT: *(angry)* That's my grandfather's money.

CLAY: Who . . . who's there?

SCOTT: You stole my grandpa's map. That money belongs to him . . . or to me.

CLAY: Who says I stole the old man's map? It's your word against mine.

NARRATOR 2:   Rico stepped from the shadows.

RICO: And my word, too, Clay. I bet that money really belongs to the bank. If we give it back, there should be some kind of reward.

SCOTT: If you stop being a jerk, maybe we'll cut you in for a share.

CLAY: Fat chance, you losers. My share is one hundred percent. Your share is zero. Now I think you two should get out of here. I've got a treasure to take home.

NARRATOR 1:   The three boys stared at each other. If it came to a fight, it would be two against one. But Clay was bigger than either Rico or Scott. He was used to beating up kids, and he knew how to use his fists.

NARRATOR 2:   Besides, Scott would be useless in a fight. The odds weren't that good, and Rico knew it. He decided to bluff.

RICO: Over my dead body.

CLAY: If that's what you want . . .

NARRATOR 1:   Clay came toward Rico with the shovel. Rico backed off into the darkness. Clay couldn't see him, but Rico was till trapped in the tunnel.

NARRATOR 2:   Scott had run to the entrance. All he could do was wait. His friend was trapped.

CLAY: I'm going to get you . . .

NARRATOR 1:   Clay smashed the shovel into the wall.

(sound effect: crash)

RICO: Missed me!

NARRATOR 2:   Clay swung again.

(sound effect: crash)

RICO: Over here, you reject.

(sound effect: crash)

RICO: Missed me again.

NARRATOR 1:   Scott was amazed. His friend was playing cat and mouse with this bully. Rico wouldn't have a hope if Clay found him.

NARRATOR 2:   Clay went back to get his flashlight. *(sound effect: footsteps)* Then he shone the light all over the tunnel. Soon he found Rico in one corner.

CLAY: *(laughing)* Now I've got you.

NARRATOR 1:   Clay lifted the shovel, but this time he hit an old wood beam.

(sound effect: crash)

RICO: Nice work, reject.

NARRATOR 2:   From above, there was a cracking sound.

(sound effect: the mine ceiling is falling down – crack)

<Three Feet Under 85>

NARRATOR 1:   Then a creaking sound.

(sound effect: creak)

NARRATOR 2:   In seconds, the ceiling of the mine began to fall!

(sound effect: crash)

RICO: Let's get out of here!

(sound effect: running footsteps, collapsing mine sound)

(closing music)

<Tag Team 87>

Tag Team

Jesse is walking home with his girlfriend, Hannah, when they are confronted by two bullies. In the fight that follows, Jesse is almost knocked cold before there is a surprising rescue.

APPROPRIATE GRADE LEVELS: 6–10

PERFORMANCE TIME: 6 minutes

THE NOVEL IN BRIEF: Jesse had plenty of problems to start with. He was short, shy and lonely – at least until he went out for the school's wrestling team. Then his life seemed to turn around, until the night he had to deal with Banjo and Joey down in the tunnel.

PERFORMING NOTES: Hannah has the major role in this play and must express a range of emotions: teasing affection, surprise and anger. Jesse begins the play cheerfully walking his girlfriend home but soon gets embroiled in a fight where his lines are reduced to grunts and groans. Banjo and Joey are the villains, sarcastic and mocking when they first appear, then belligerent. Joey's role is small but important. Sound effects, though there are many of them, can be done by the student actors themselves.

Narrator 1 (10 lines)
Narrator 2 (10 lines)
Jesse – a short high school wrestler (13 lines)
Hannah – Jesse's girlfriend (16 lines)
Banjo Girard – a bully, also a wrestler (10 lines)
Joey – Banjo's friend (5 lines)

SOUND EFFECTS: *fight sounds: thump, crunch, groan; running footsteps, slamming door*

<88 Tag Team>

Tag Team – Readers' Theater

Narrator 1
Narrator 2
Jesse – a short high school wrestler
Hannah – Jesse's girlfriend
Banjo Girard – a bully, also a wrestler
Joey – Banjo's friend

SOUND EFFECTS: *fight sounds: thump, crunch, groan; running steps, slamming door*

NARRATOR 1: This Readers' Theater play is adapted from the novel *Tag Team* by Paul Kropp. Today's actors are

_____

_____

_____

NARRATOR 2: Jesse and Hannah had a great time when they went out together. Jesse was surprised. He wasn't funny or smart or cool, but that didn't seem to matter.

NARRATOR 1: Hannah just seemed to like him.

NARRATOR 2: One day, Hannah met Jesse after a rehearsal at school. She had a lead role in the school's musical, *Pirates of Penzance*.

JESSE: You're a really good actress, and a good singer, too.

HANNAH: *(laughing)* Not a really good singer?

JESSE: *(embarrassed)* Well, you're acting is great and your singing . . .

HANNAH: It's only okay. I know that, Jes. But my voice is good enough for a school musical.

JESSE: Oh, your singing is much better than that. I think you're going to be a star.

HANNAH: You've just got stars in your eyes.

JESSE: No, that's not it. I mean, maybe I do have stars in my eyes, but you're so good you could be on TV.

HANNAH: I'd rather be on Broadway, if you don't mind.

NARRATOR 1: Jesse took Hannah's hand and the two of them walked down the street.

NARRATOR 2: Soon they were walking through the tunnel under Lewin Parkway. That's when they saw Banjo Girard down at the end of the tunnel. He was talking with his friend Joey.

NARRATOR 1: Banjo looked up at Jesse and Hannah.

BANJO: Well, look who's here . . . and holding hands!

JOEY: That's one way to make the wrestling team. Just go out with the coach's daughter. Works every time! *(Joey and Banjo laugh)*

BANJO: No other way a shrimp like Jes could make the team.

JOEY: He's so small the other guys can't even see him. I heard a guy at the last meet talking about it. He said, "Hey, why's this little guy holding my knees?" *(more laughter)*

JESSE: *(angry)* Why don't you two shut your traps?

BANJO: Hey, the little guy sounds scary.

JOEY: The shrimp is angry.

BANJO: *(sarcastic)* I'm so-o afraid! *(more laughter)*

<90 Tag Team>

HANNAH: Come on, Jes. Let's go the other way. These idiots aren't worth talking to.

BANJO: Listen to her, trying to protect the little guy. She's always having to look after the shrimp.

JOEY: Hey, Banjo, why do you think she's going out with a little guy like that?

BANJO: Well, I think she's gotta be pretty hard up. Or maybe she's a loser, just like he is. *(more laughter)*

NARRATOR 2:   That when Jesse lost it. It was one thing for the guys to insult him. It was something else when they picked on his girlfriend.

NARRATOR 1:   Jesse ran at the two of them, then jumped at Banjo, swinging with his right fist. But Banjo fell back and Jesse didn't connect.

BANJO: Hey, little man, you're not much of a fighter. I bet you're not much of a wrestler, either.

NARRATOR 2:   That made Jesse even angrier. He lunged at Banjo, trying to get a wrestling hold. But this fight wasn't like wrestling in the gym.

NARRATOR 1:   Banjo just slugged him in the stomach.

JESSE: *(groan of pain)*

BANJO: *(mocking)* Come on, little guy. Let's see you wrestle some more.

HANNAH: Jes, stop it!

NARRATOR 2:   Jesse didn't listen to her. Instead, he charged into Banjo with his shoulder. The big guy cried out in pain.

BANJO: *(grunt)*

NARRATOR 1: Then Jesse grabbed Banjo's arm. He flipped the big guy over his shoulder and down to the concrete. *(sound effect: thump)*

BANJO: I'm gonna kill you.

JESSE: Give it up, Banjo. That's enough.

NARRATOR 2: But Banjo wasn't going to stop the fight. He nodded to Joey, who got behind Jesse. With a quick move, Joey knocked Jes to the ground.

HANNAH: Hey, that's not fair.

NARRATOR 1: Jesse was still down when Banjo punched him in the jaw. *(sound effect: grunt)* Then a second punch hit Jesse right in his gut. *(sound effect: grunt)*

NARRATOR 2: One more punch would have knocked Jesse cold. But that punch never came.

HANNAH: Stop it! I said stop it!

NARRATOR 1: Hannah's knee came up and connected with Banjo's jaw. *(sound effect: crunch)* His big body fell on the cement and didn't move. *(sound effect: thump)*

HANNAH: What about you, Joey?

JOEY: Hey, we're cool, Hannah. I didn't mean nothing. Really, nothing at all. *(sound effect: running footsteps)*

NARRATOR 2: Hannah reached down and helped Jesse to his feet.

JESSE: How did you . . . ?

HANNAH: Five years of Karate lessons when I was little. I never thought I'd have to use that stuff, but I guess you never know. Come on. Let's get out of here before that idiot gets up.

<92 Tag Team>

NARRATOR 1: Jesse and Hannah didn't have much to say on the walk home. Jesse still hurt from the fight. And Hannah was angry.

NARRATOR 2: When they got to Hannah's door, she finally blew up.

HANNAH: That whole thing was stupid, Jes. It was stupid, stupid, stupid!

JESSE: But you heard what he said about you.

HANNAH: You think I can't handle a couple of crude comments? Or that I need to you play Superman? You've got the team finals in a week, and look at you. Here, take a Kleenex and clean your face.

JESSE: I just –

HANNAH: I don't want to hear it. If I told my father about this, you'd be cut from the team – just like that.

JESSE: You wouldn't.

HANNAH: I don't know what I'm going to do. Maybe it serves me right going out with a wrestler. I thought you were special, but you guys are all the same – you all think that fighting can solve something.

JESSE: Hannah, please.

HANNAH: I can't believe that I ended up in a fight, that you dragged me down to that level.

JESSE: But Hannah, there was nothing –

HANNAH: It was stupid, Jesse. And I've had enough. Please don't call me again. Not tonight . . . not ever.

(sound effect: door slamming)

(closing music)

<Street Scene 93>

Street Scene

A gang of white kids chase Jamal and Sammy through the back alleys of the city. At the end, Jamal is trapped.

APPROPRIATE GRADE LEVELS: 6–12

PERFORMANCE TIME: 4 minutes

THE NOVEL IN BRIEF: A group of black teens defend themselves against harassment from a white gang. Violence escalates, with tragic results.

PERFORMING NOTES: Sound effects are quite essential to this play and should be given to a student who does not otherwise have a role. (Note that there is a great deal of running and heavy breathing as the play goes on.) There are no narrator roles in this script; instead the story is told by Jamal and Sammy. They have to switch from description to action as the story unfolds. The characters of Sal and Marco are your basic "hoods" and fairly easy to portray.

Jamal – an African-American teen (12 lines)
Sammy – Jamal's friend, same age (6 lines)
Sal – leader of a gang (8 lines)
Marco – Sal's buddy (7 lines)

SOUND EFFECTS: *car screeching, footsteps, grunting, police siren, slamming car doors, bouncing basketball, crashing garbage cans, wood smashing against metal*

<94 Street Scene>

Street Scene – Readers' Theater

Jamal – a teenage boy
Sammy – Jamal's friend, same age
Sal – leader of a gang
Marco – Sal's buddy

SOUND EFFECTS: *car screeching, footsteps, grunting, police siren, slamming car doors, bouncing basketball, crashing garbage cans, wood smashing against metal*

ANY CHARACTER: This Readers' Theater play is adapted from *Street Scene* by Paul Kropp. Today's actors are

_____

_____

_____

JAMAL: The thing about trouble is that it shows up when it wants to – not when you're ready for it. That's what my mom says. And maybe she's right. When the trouble came to us, we weren't thinking about it. We were thinking about basketball. *(sound effect: bouncing basketball)*

SAMMY: Jamal and I were just walking down the street, going to the Rec Center. I guess we were joking around too, about those "tough" west end guys. Those guys hadn't done nothing to us for three days now. It all seemed like a big laugh . . . until a car zoomed up beside us.

<Street Scene 95>

(sound effect: car screeching to a halt, car doors opening and closing)

JAMAL: Three guys got out. The first two guys were just your average greaseballs. They were all bigger than me and Sammy, but they didn't look too smart or too fast.

SAMMY: I figured that we could either deke out those guys or outrun them if we had to. Then Sal climbed out of the car *(sound effect: car doors, footsteps)* and I started to sweat a little.

SAL: So look who's here. Must be Jamal and his little friend Sammy.

MARCO: Just the guys we were looking for. *(Sal and Marco laugh)*

SAMMY: Somebody jabbed me in the side, so I said, "Hey, man! What you doing?" But Jamal didn't want to wait around.

JAMAL: Let's get out of here!

SAMMY: So I ran one way and Jamal went the other way. Jamal had three guys chasing him. I just had the guy in the car.

(sound effect: running footsteps – two boys first, then one, then the rest of the gang)

JAMAL: *(out of breath)* Got to use my brain. Got to get away from these guys. I jumped over a fence and tried to get clear.

(sound effect: racing footsteps)

SAL: *(breathing hard)* Hey man. Don't think you can get away that easy.

MARCO: You see him?

<96 Street Scene>

SAL: He had to go this way!

(sound effect: more running, crashing garbage cans)

JAMAL: I knew I couldn't get away from those guys, so I had to hide. I squeezed between two sheds and waited. *(breathing hard)* I picked up a piece of wood, for insurance.

(sound effect: footsteps, running, then slowing down)

MARCO: He's got be around here someplace.

SAL: Check between the sheds. I think I hear something.

JAMAL: I was trying not to make noise. I would have stopped breathing if I could. But still they found me.

MARCO: Well, look who's here.

SAL: We've got you now, Jamal. *(laughter)*

JAMAL: *(scared)* Stay back, man.

(sound effect: wood smashing against metal)

SAL: Tough guy, eh? Marco, give him a poke with that old pipe. We'll see how tough this guy is.

JAMAL: Marco began to jab at me.

MARCO: Come on out, guy. We're waiting for you.

SAL: Now we got you!

JAMAL: I tried to swing at them with my piece of wood, but Sal grabbed it. In a flash, Sal punched me in the side. *(Jamal grunts.)* Then Marco got ready to take a swing at me.

MARCO: This is for you, boy.

<Street Scene 97>

JAMAL: This is the end – that's what I thought to myself. I'm never going to get up after they get through with me. *(pause)* But then I heard something.

(sound effect: police siren coming closer, slamming doors)

SAL: It's the cops!

MARCO: Let's get out of here!

SAMMY: Sal and Marco tried to run, but the police had blocked the alley. They were trapped. As the cops rounded up the gang, I walked up to Jamal.

(sound effect: footsteps)

JAMAL: *(still scared)* Sammy, is that you?

SAMMY: Yeah, man. I lost my guy, then I figured you might need a little help.

JAMAL: You figured right. Sometimes a little help is a real good thing. *(laughter)*

(closing music)

<Student Narc 99>

Student Narc

Kevin is lured to see the Candyman, a drug dealer, and gets accused of being a narc.

APPROPRIATE GRADE LEVELS: 7–12

PERFORMANCE TIME: 3-1/2 minutes

THE NOVEL IN BRIEF: A student goes undercover to bust a drug gang and avenge his best friend's death.

PERFORMING NOTES: In the novel, this scene leads to the final escape by Kevin and to the police shooting the Goon and Candyman. As a result, this script ends with a kind of ominous foreshadowing. Kevin does most of the real acting. Dawn is drugged and tearful for much of the script. Buddy, the Candyman and the Goon can all be played as typical Hollywood villains. Sound effects are relatively unimportant.

This play can be staged if your students can memorize a sufficient number of the lines. The narration can be cut or read from the sidelines.

Narrator 1
Narrator 2
Kevin – the hero, working for the police to avenge his friend's death
Dawn – drug user involved in the gang
Buddy – a middle-ranking drug dealer
The Candyman – boss of the drug gang
Goon – a bad guy in the drug gang

SOUND EFFECTS: *car door closing, car screeching to a stop, knocking on the door, door slamming, a struggle, footsteps*

<100 Student Narc>

Student Narc – Readers' Theater

Narrator 1
Narrator 2
Kevin – the hero, working undercover for the police
Dawn   drug user involved in the gang
Buddy – a middle-ranking drug dealer
The Candyman – boss of the drug gang
Goon – a goon

SOUND EFFECTS: *car door closing, car screeching to a stop, knocking on the door, door slamming, a struggle, footsteps*

NARRATOR 1:   This Readers' Theater play is adapted from novel *Student Narc* by Paul Kropp. Today's actors are

_____

_____

_____

NARRATOR 2:   In the story so far, Kevin has begun to work undercover for the police. He's out to nail the Candyman – a drug dealer who may have killed Kevin's best friend.

NARRATOR 1:   At midnight, Kevin got a call from Dawn – a girl involved in the drug gang. She wanted to see him right away.

NARRATOR 2:   Kevin met Dawn at her car and climbed inside. *(sound effect: car door closing)*

KEVIN: Hey, Dawn, what's the matter?

DAWN: It's Buddy. He wants to see you at the apartment.

<Student Narc 101>

KEVIN: At midnight?

DAWN: Yeah, like right away.

NARRATOR 1: Kevin was nervous. The police had given him a wire to wear, but he left it back at the house.

KEVIN: I thought *you* wanted to talk. I mean, I'm not real happy seeing Buddy in the middle of the night. I've got school tomorrow.

DAWN: *(cold voice)* He told me to bring you. *(She begins to sniffle.)*

KEVIN: Dawn . . . are you okay?

DAWN: Yes . . . no . . . oh, I don't know.

(sound effect: Dawn's car screeches to a stop)

DAWN: We better go upstairs. Buddy's been waiting for you.

NARRATOR 2: Dawn led Kevin up to Buddy's apartment. They knocked at the door. *(sound effect: knocking on door)*

BUDDY: Hey, nice to see you, Kevin.

KEVIN: Hey, Buddy. What's this all about?

BUDDY: I hear you wanted to meet somebody, so this must be your lucky night. Come on in, guy. This is the Candyman.

NARRATOR 1: Kevin knew he was in trouble. There were three men in the apartment: Buddy, the Candyman and a goon with greasy hair. The goon moved behind Kevin as the door slammed shut. *(sound effect: door slamming)*

CANDYMAN: Search him! *(sound effect: struggle)*

GOON: He's clean.

<102 Student Narc>

BUDDY: Okay, let's get to it. Kevin, who are you working for?

KEVIN: I'm not working for anybody.

GOON: *(sarcastic)* Yeah, right! I told you the kid was a plant.

CANDYMAN: He suckered you in, Buddy.

BUDDY: Look, I found out soon enough, didn't I? We've got him here, don't we?

CANDYMAN: You working for the cops, kid?

NARRATOR 2: The goon kept twisting Kevin's arm. He looked as if he wanted to take Kevin apart.

KEVIN: *(in pain)* I don't know anything. Look, you've got some problem with Buddy, it doesn't have anything to do with me. I did a little deal with him, that's all. Just let me out of here and you do what you want.

BUDDY: Nice try, Kevin, but it won't work. We checked with your friend Birney. He says he never bought that baby jar from you. He says he never bought nothing from you.

GOON: Now what's the real story, kid?

NARRATOR 1: The goon grabbed Kevin by the neck and began to choke him.

KEVIN: *(choking)* Birney's lying! He asked me to make the deal and get him the stuff – I swear it!

BUDDY: And Birney swears that he's telling the truth. You're the guy who doesn't add up, Kevin. You come over from Tech and then move in on Dawn. A week later, you make some phony deal with me. Then, all of a sudden, there's a bug on my car.

<Student Narc 103>

CANDYMAN: It all stinks, kid. But maybe you'll open up when you see what comes next. Come on, we're all going for a ride.

NARRATOR 2: On the couch, Dawn was shaking and crying – coming down off drugs. *(sound effect: crying)* She was in no shape to help anyone. Kevin was desperate.

KEVIN: Are you going to kill me like you did Matt?

BUDDY: Sort of, except your friend shot the stuff into his own arm. Besides, you've got some stuff to tell us first. Then we'll figure out what to do with you.

CANDYMAN: And if you don't talk, we might have to kill your little girlfriend first.

NARRATOR 1: The goon grabbed Kevin with one hand, shoving his gun into Kevin's back. Buddy grabbed Dawn.

NARRATOR 2: Then the five of them began moving slowly down the hall. *(sound effect: footsteps)*

(ominous closing music)

<Juvie 105>

Juvie

This play tells the story of a breakout from a juvenile detention center. It is tense and violent and not for younger readers.

APPROPRIATE GRADE LEVELS: 7–12

PERFORMANCE TIME: 4 minutes

THE NOVEL IN BRIEF: A gripping story of the harsh life inside a juvenile detention center. Russ has been sent to Juvie for a crime he didn't commit. What he sees there opens his eyes to the darker aspects of life.

PERFORMING NOTES: Russ is the narrator of the novel and a relatively unhardened inmate of a juvenile detention center. Sig is very on edge, willing to do anything to escape. To be effective, both roles require some serious acting. Sound effects are very important and will require the full attention of one student.

We recommend that Russ' decision at the end of the play be discussed with the class. He is legally in the wrong when he helps Sig to escape, but given the situation in the novel, the moral issues are open for discussion.

Narrator 1 (11 lines)
Narrator 2 (11 lines)
Russ – an inmate at a juvenile detention center (13 lines)
Sig – another inmate, desperate to escape (14 lines)
Voice of a staff guard (through a megaphone)

SOUND EFFECTS: *footsteps, fire alarm, siren, smashing door, heavy breathing*

<106 Juvie>

Juvie – Readers' Theater

Narrator 1
Narrator 2
Russ – an inmate at a juvenile detention center
Sig – another inmate, desperate to escape
Voice of a staff guard

SOUND EFFECTS: *footsteps, fire alarm, siren, smashing door*

NARRATOR 1: This Readers' Theater play is adapted from *Juvie* by Paul Kropp. Today's actors are

_____

_____

_____

NARRATOR 2: Sig was desperate to escape from Juvie. The first part of his plan was to take a hostage. At first, Sig grabbed Jenna, one of the girls. Russ convinced him to let her go. Then Russ became the hostage.

NARRATOR 1: Sig started a paper fire in the wastebasket. When the alarm went off, Sig grabbed Russ around the neck. He dragged Russ sideways down the hall.

RUSS: *(choking)* Hey, let go of me. I promise I won't take off on you. We can go faster if you let me walk.

SIG: You're the hostage, Russ. You're going to make sure I get out of here.

RUSS: Yeah, but I'm a better hostage if I can breathe. If you need a shield or something, grab me. Otherwise, let me go.

SIG: Can I trust you?

<Juvie 107>

RUSS: You've got to trust somebody, Sig. I've got no reason to turn you in.

NARRATOR 2: Sig let go of Russ's neck. Then the two of them ran down the tunnel. *(sound effect: footsteps running)*

NARRATOR 1: The fire alarm was ringing as they ran. *(sound effect: fire alarm)* At the far end of the tunnel was a door to the front hall. Beyond that was one more door, the door leading outside.

NARRATOR 2: The front hall door was locked, but Gracie's pass-card got it open. But the last door was locked and stayed locked. The guys in the control room had figured out Sig's plan.

NARRATOR 1: Sig grabbed Russ again. Then he shouted at a security camera.

SIG: *(shouting)* Open the door or I'll cut him.

NARRATOR 2: Russ could fee the knife blade. It was cold against his neck.

SIG: Open it!

NARRATOR 1: But nothing happened. The door stayed locked.

RUSS: *(scared)* Listen, Sig, it doesn't pay to cut me. Those guys in the control room don't care. I'll end up bleeding. And you'll just end up in the pen.

SIG: Okay, we'll go to Plan B.

RUSS: Plan B?

SIG: Yeah, man. Any guy with half a brain knows you need a Plan B.

NARRATOR 2: The two of them ran back into the tunnel. *(sound effect: running footsteps)* When they got halfway, Sig stopped and ran against a metal door. *(sound effect: smash)*

<108 Juvie>

NARRATOR 1:   The door burst open.

RUSS: How'd you do that?

SIG: I cut the lock last week when I was on yard duty. Just in case.

NARRATOR 2:   It was cold, wet and foggy when they popped out of the tunnel. They could still hear the fire alarm, but now there was a new sound – the escape siren. *(sound effect: siren)*

RUSS: What now?

SIG: To the fence, man.

NARRATOR 1:   Sig ran along the fence until he found a storm sewer. It was half filled from the rain, but a guy could still squeeze through it.

RUSS: Not bad, Sig. I like your Plan B.

SIG: There's a car out there, waiting. So are you coming with me?

RUSS: I can't do it, Sig. I'm too gutless.

SIG: Last chance, Russ. I got a buddy out there.

NARRATOR 2:   Sig might have said more, but they could both hear voices and running steps coming closer. *(sound effect: footsteps)*

VOICE: *(muffled, at a distance)* Give it up, kid.

SIG: *(shouting)* Don't come closer. You come closer and Russ starts to bleed.

NARRATOR 1:   The fog was very thick. Sig couldn't see the staff guys. Nor could the staff see him.

VOICE: Let Russ go.

<Juvie 109>

SIG: No way. You start anything and you'll have a dead body here. Try to explain that one. We all know how you suckered Jackson and the D-wing guys. You think you can get away with that twice?

NARRATOR 1: It was quiet. The only sound was the siren and the guys' heavy breathing. *(sound effects: siren, breathing)*

SIG: *(whispering)* Start talking to them.

RUSS: *(whispering)* And say what?

SIG: *(whispering)* Anything, man. Just give me some time to get out of here.

NARRATOR 2: Sig went quietly into the storm sewer.

VOICE: What's going on there?

RUSS: *(shouting)* He's got a knife at my throat. He says he'll kill me if you come any closer. Why don't you let Sig go? He didn't hurt anybody back there.

VOICE: Sig, we're going to give you ten seconds to let Russ go. Ten seconds.

NARRATOR 1: Russ didn't like this. What were they going to do in ten seconds? Would they come in shooting?

VOICE: Nine . . . eight . . . seven.

NARRATOR 2: Russ knew that Sig would be getting to the road by now. Soon he'd be getting into his buddy's car.

NARRATOR 1: Sig always wanted to escape. Now he was almost free.

VOICE: Six . . . five . . . four . . . Let him go, Sig.

RUSS: It's okay! He put the knife down!

VOICE: Then walk toward us, both of you. No funny stuff.

<110 Juvie>

NARRATOR 2: Slowly Russ walked toward the voice. *(sound effect: slow footsteps)* He was trying to give Sig as much time as he could. At last he could see the staff guys, waiting.

VOICE: Where'd he go? Where's Sig?

RUSS: *(acting innocent)* Beats me. He was right behind me a second ago.

(Closing music)

HIP Sr. Novels

READING LEVEL: 3.0–4.0   INTEREST LEVELS: Grades 4–12

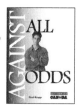

AGAINST ALL ODDS *by Paul Kropp.*
A special student risks his life to gain the respect of his older brother. Reading level: grade 3.4, Interest level: grades 6–10

GHOST HOUSE *by Paul Kropp.*
Three boys spend a night in a haunted house. Reading level: grade 3.2, Interest level: grades 4–10

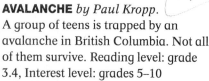

AVALANCHE *by Paul Kropp.*
A group of teens is trapped by an avalanche in British Columbia. Not all of them survive. Reading level: grade 3.4, Interest level: grades 5–10

HACKER *by Alex Kropp.*
A computer whiz and a football player fight computer crime at their school. Reading level: grade 3.6, Interest level: grades 4–9

THE BULLY *by Liz Brown.*
A teenage girl struggles against lies and rumors spread by a girl at her school. Reading level: grade 3.2, Interest level: grades 4–9

HITTING THE ROAD *by Paul Kropp.*
A young teen and his best friend run away from home. Reading level: grade 3.2, Interest level: grades 6–12

CAUGHT IN THE BLIZZARD
by Paul Kropp.
Three teenagers in the Arctic deal with rivalry and crime, and then must survive a winter storm. Reading level: grade 4.0, Interest level: grades 5–12

JUVIE *by Paul Kropp.*
A dramatic story of attempted escape from a juvenile detention center. Reading level: grade 2.8 Interest level: grades 5–10

DARK RYDER *by Liz Brown.*
A teenage girl must train and ride a wild horse in order to keep him. Reading level: grade 4.0, Interest level: grades 4–9

THE KID IS LOST! *by Paul Kropp.*
A missing child forces two teens to a search with ATVs through a deadly swamp. Reading level: grade 3.6, Interest level: grades 6–10

FOUL SHOT *by Paul Kropp*
The Cougars haven't won a game in years, but Luther sees a way to break the losing streak. But not quite for the whole season. Reading level: grade 3.0, Interest level: grades 4–10

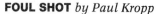

MY BROKEN FAMILY *by Paul Kropp.*
A girl learns that her parents' divorce is not quite as terrible as she had thought. Reading level: grade 3.8, Interest level: grades 5–10

ONE CRAZY NIGHT *by Paul Kropp.*
Adventures and misadventures of a teenage boy working at a small-town deli-gas station. Reading level: grade 3.8, Interest level: grades 6–10

OUR PLANE IS DOWN! *by Doug Paton.*
A small plane goes down in the bush, hours from anywhere, and two teens must fight to survive and rescue the pilot. Reading level: grade 4.0, Interest level: grades 4–10

PLAYING CHICKEN *by Paul Kropp.*
Drinking, driving and drugs lead to tragedy when a group of teenagers try to run a rail crossing. Reading level: grade 3.6, Interest level: grades 6–12

RUNNING FOR DAVE *by Lori Jamison.*
When a track star gets cancer, his best friend finds new meaning for his own life. Reading level: grade 3.2, Interest level: grades 6–10

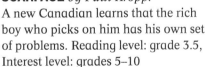

SCARFACE *by Paul Kropp.*
A new Canadian learns that the rich boy who picks on him has his own set of problems. Reading level: grade 3.5, Interest level: grades 5–10

SHOLA'S GAME *by Shawn Durkin.*
A recent immigrant finds that hockey helps him fit into his new country. Reading level: grade 3.4, Interest level: grades 4–9

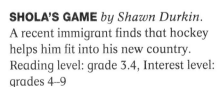

SHOW OFF *by Paul Kropp.*
A teenage girl finally rejects the crazy vandalism of her friends. Reading level: grade 3.8, Interest level: grades 5–10

STEALING HOME *by Shawn Durkin.*
Josh is trying to fit in with the guys, trying to make his way in a new school. Baseball is the one thing he does really well, but his best friend on the school team is leading him into dangerous territory. Reading level: grade 3.2, Interest level: grades 4–10

STREET SCENE *by Paul Kropp.*
A group of black teens in Toronto defend themselves against harassment from a gang, with tragic results. Reading level: grade 4.0, Interest level: grades 6–12

STUDENT NARC *by Paul Kropp.*
A student goes undercover to avenge his best friend's death. Reading level: grade 3.8, Interest level: grades 5–10

TAG TEAM *by Paul Kropp.*
A small high school student goes out for his school's wrestling team and finds that size doesn't matter. Reading level: grade 3.5, Interest level: grades 4–10

TERROR 9/11 *by Doug Paton.*
A teenage boy and his sister survive the collapse of the World Trade Center. Reading level: grade 3.5, Interest level: grades 5–10

HIP Jr. Novels

READING LEVEL: 2.0–2.5   INTEREST LEVELS: Grades 3–6

BATS PAST MIDNIGHT
by Sharon Jennings
First book in the Bat series: Sam and Simon (the Bat Gang) wonder about a fancy car that hangs around their school late at night. When they try to find out more, they end up in trouble at school, at home and with the police.

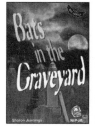

BATS IN THE GRAVEYARD
by Sharon Jennings
Second book in the Bat series: Sam and Simon have to look after Sam's little sister on Halloween night. Soon the Bats end up in the graveyard, chased by a ghoul and falling into an open grave. And then it all gets worse!

JINGLE BATS
by Sharon Jennings
Third book in the Bat series: Sam and Simon get holiday jobs at the local mall working as Santa's elves. But when toys start to disappear from the donation box, the Bat Gang has to find the thief!

CHOOSE YOUR BULLY
by Lori Jamison
Ling and Richard have a great idea to deal with their school bully – hire a bodyguard. But when their bodyguard starts to bully them too, they have to get even smarter.

THE CRASH *by Paul Kropp*
A school bus slides down a cliff in a snowstorm. The bus driver is out cold. One of the guys is badly hurt. Can Craig, Rory and Lerch find help in time?

I DIDN'T DO IT
by Paul Kropp
Tom has just moved to the big city and left all his old friends behind. Now he's getting blamed for strange things that take place at his new school. Somebody is trying to make him look guilty. And Tom has to get smart, fast, in order to clear his name.

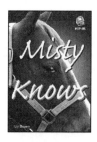

MISTY KNOWS *by Liz Brown*
Someone is putting poison in the feed at the stable. Jen and Keisha have an idea who's behind it, but finding proof gets them in serious trouble.

PUMP! *by Sharon Jennings*
Pat's tired of getting hassled by neighbors about his skateboarding. He wants a skateboard park so he can work on his skills. But Pat learns that getting a park is harder than he ever expected.

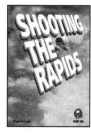

SHOOTING THE RAPIDS
by Paul Kropp
When their dad gets hurt on a canoe trip, it's up to two brothers to get him back to town. But Connor and Timmy soon get lost in the wilderness. Can they reach help in time to save their father?

THREE FEET UNDER
by Paul Kropp
Scott and Rico find a map to long-lost treasure. There's $250,000 buried in Bolton's mine. But when the school bully steals their map and tries to beat them to it, the race is on.

High Interest Publishing – Publishers of H·I·P Books
407 Wellesley Street East | Toronto, Ontario M4X 1H5
www.hip-books.com | 416.323.3710 | hip-books@sympatico.ca

An imprint of the Chestnut Publishing Group: www.chesnutpublishing.com

19.95
9.95